Bring the Full Tithe

Bring the Full Tithe
Sermons on the Grace of Giving

William D. Watley

Judson Press ® Valley Forge

Bring the Full Tithe: Sermons on the Grace of Giving
© 1995
Judson Press, Valley Forge, PA 19482-0851

Unless otherwise indicated, Scripture quotations in this volume are from the Revised Standard Version of the Bible, copyright © 1946, 1952, 1971, by the Division of Christian Education of the National Council of the Churches of Christ in the USA. Used by permission. (RSV) Other Scripture quotations are from the New Revised Standard Version of the Bible, copyright 1989 by the Division of Christian Education of the National Council of the Churches of Christ in the United States of America, and are used by permission. All rights reserved. (NRSV) *The Holy Bible*, King James Version (KJV); and the HOLY BIBLE: *New International Version*, copyright © 1973, 1978, 1984. Used by permission of Zondervan Bible Publishers. (NIV)

Library of Congress Cataloging-in-Publication Data
Watley, William D.
    Bring the full tithe: sermons on the grace of giving/ William D. Watley.
    p. cm.
    Includes bibliographical references.
    ISBN 0-8170-1230-3
    1. Tithes—Sermons. 2. Stewardship, Christian—Sermons. 3. African Methodist Episcopal Church—Sermons. 4. Methodist Church—Sermons. 5. Sermons, American. I. Title.
    BV772.W36 1995
    248'.6—dc20   94-40295

Printed in the U.S.A.

99 00 01 02   8 7 6 5 4

Contents

Preface

This book has been in embryonic form in my spirit for close to a decade. Ever since I saw in my own life and ministry how tithing can transform a church, the lives of those laypersons who practice it, and those preachers who proclaim as well as practice, I have wanted to write a book of sermons on stewardship and tithing. I am grateful for the opportunity to do so.

I have seen what tithing can do in terms of a congregation's personality, spirituality, and sense of mission. When a church spends an inordinate amount of time and attention on fund-raising just to survive rather than on strengthening the saints and keeping ahead, on maintenance rather than mission, and on paying bills rather than preaching Christ, then that church is unable to really be the church.

Two examples emerge from my childhood of ministries that were excellent paradigms of spirituality and stewardship, mission and money, teaching and tithing. The first example is a servant of the Lord to whom I affectionately refer as Uncle Grady. To the rest of the world he is known as the Reverend Grady R. Brown, pastor of the First African Methodist Episcopal (A.M.E.) Church in Kansas City, Kansas. Uncle Grady was the first person to teach me that we tithe from our gross total income and not simply from our net salary. His gifts as a preacher, his humble spirit, his lifestyle of simplicity, and his uncompromising commitment to tithing as the word of God for the support of the church, all balanced by his true shepherd's heart, make him a role model par excellence. The accomplishments of his ministry based solely on giving rather than fund-raising are noteworthy. This book is dedicated to the life and ministry of Uncle Grady.

The second paradigm from my childhood of exemplary steward-ship and tithing is the Reverend Frank C. Cummings, who is now a bishop in the African Methodist Episcopal church. During my childhood Bishop Cummings was the pastor of St. John A.M.E. Church in St. Louis, Missouri. Under his leadership and unswerving commitment to freeing the people of God to do mission by support-ing the church only through tithes and offerings, a struggling inner-city congregation became a vibrant community of faith, known for what it did for others. While he was pastor of St. John, the offering plate was not even passed on Sunday morning as part of the regular routine. People brought their gifts to the altar and deposited them in the receptacle as they knelt to pray. Thus people truly worshiped, rather than talked and walked, as they gave.

Both Uncle Grady and Bishop Cummings set examples for me that I am still trying to reach. My present bishop, the Right Reverend Philip R. Cousin, is also an excellent example and model of sound, sensible, sane, and solid biblical stewardship in terms of his per-sonal giving and teaching.

This book, like all the others that I have written and read, is a collaborative effort. Let me express my appreciation to my sister and friend, Mrs. Carolyn Scavella, for her editing skills as well as her pointed and challenging questions, which helped to clarify my own thinking. I am also indebted to Ms. Louise Warren, my com-petent, congenial, and caring office administrator who typed 95 percent of the manuscript from my handwritten text, which some have compared to hieroglyphics. I am grateful to her and to my son-in-law, Charles Maxell, for patiently and painstakingly teach-ing me how to use WordPerfect for the 5 percent that I struggled to type.

My wife, Muriel, is always deserving of special mention. She has heard me preach more often than any other person alive. I am sure that over the last twenty-six years that we have been married she has heard more about tithing than she ever wanted to know. She has been a blessing to my life and ministry, and I continue to be grateful for her faithfulness.

Last but certainly not least, I praise God for the privilege of shepherding the good and gracious, sincere and saved, strong and Spirit-filled people of St. James A.M.E. Church in Newark, New Jersey. Without their love for the Word of God and their willingness to receive and apply it to their own lives, as well as their cooperative spirit and openness to leadership and change, the sermons in this book would have been as seed sown in stony ground and among weeds. They have been good soil for the message of tithing to take root, grow, flourish, and yield an abundant crop.

1. Preparing the Soil for the Seed

Introduction

When I was around six or eight years old, my parents told me that they were going to start giving me an allowance of twenty-five cents per week. Naturally I was happy to hear that I was going to be receiving a whole quarter every week. However, I had never heard the word *allowance* before, and thus I was appropriately confused regarding its purpose. My parents explained that I was to purchase my small daily needs and wants, such as potato chips, ice cream soda, trinkets, and so on, from my allowance. No longer was I to ask them for spending change. My miscellaneous wants *(wants* as I understand them now, *needs* as I felt about them then) were to come from my allowance. I would have to make my allowance last from one week to the next because nothing more would be forthcoming. (Of course, there were exceptions to what first appeared as a hard-and-fast rule, permanently etched in stone. Thank God for mercy as well as justice!)

I was also told that a nickel from my allowance was to be set aside for church. There was no discussion on either the instructions that my church money was to come from my allowance or the amount. The nickel to the church was as much a given as was the amount of the allowance. Without my knowing it, I was being taught the basic lesson of Christian stewardship: the Lord and the church have a claim on whatever resources an individual may have. Stated another way, the lesson I was being taught was that a person is to set aside something for the Lord and the church out of whatever resources he or she may have.

When I reflect on the fact that a nickel out of twenty-five cents was church money, I realize I was further being taught the lesson that church money, or the Lord's money, should be a generous rather than niggardly portion of one's resources. The fact that a nickel from my allowance was unquestionably to go to the church meant that church money—the Lord's money—should not be an afterthought. Our gift to the Lord should be a priority in our lives. The first question we need ask ourselves when we look at our resources is the age-old question of the psalmist: "What shall I return to the LORD for all his bounty to me?" (Psalm 116:12, NRSV).

Although I was taught to give a generous portion of my resources since the time I was given that allowance, I have been consciously tithing since I was about fourteen years old. Around that time my father began to expand and increase his teaching and preaching on tithing (the biblically based practice of giving 10 percent of one's resources as the minimum gift to the Lord). Since my early teenage years, tithing has been endemic to my praxis as a follower of Jesus Christ as Lord and Savior. Thus I am a committed, lifetime tither. I am excited about tithing! I personally enjoy bringing my tithes and offerings to the Lord in his storehouse, which for me is the church.

When one is excited about something, one can mistakenly assume that others will share the joy. Sometimes our zeal for an idea, concept, or vision will outrun our knowledge of human nature. As a pastor, I have often made the painful discovery that one's vision is just that—one's vision. In other words, just because the Lord shows you a vision doesn't mean that the Lord has shown the same vision to your constituency.

This painful realization came to me the first time I tried to preach a tithing series in my congregation. I am privileged to pastor a warm, loyal, loving congregation of believers. Our worship services are usually Spirit-filled and inspiring. The response to my first sermon on tithing, however, was far from awesome. *Awful* would be a more appropriate expression. Saints who shouted and rejoiced on a regular basis were silent and sullen that Sunday. Even the little children seemed to be less friendly and more reticent about hugging the shepherd whom they had showered with so much affection heretofore. As I recall the experience, it was as if an iceberg akin to the one that had sunk the Titanic had landed in the congregation. As a matter of fact, for a moment I thought I had hit the same iceberg and that I was sinking, never to rise again. There was not a lot of hostility, but the silence was deafening and the response, bone chilling. To put the matter succinctly, I discovered that a number of my members did not share my enthusiasm for tithing.

As I prepared this collection of sermons on stewardship and tithing, it occurred to me that an introductory chapter about the red flags and mine fields to which one should be sensitive in initiating a tithing program in a congregation or teaching tithing to believers may be helpful. That is the purpose of this first chapter. My prayer is that the insights gained through my experience, as I have tried to be a responsible and concerned shepherd by teaching stewardship and tithing to the flock of Christ, will be helpful to others engaged in such a ministry.

The Preacher's Closet Preparation

If the maximum stewardship results are to be achieved in terms of Christian nurture, growth, and discipleship, the preacher (or other presenter) must be prepared. No preacher or presenter should ever face the people of God poorly prepared or unprepared. To do so at any time is disgraceful, and to do so vis-à-vis stewardship and tithing is disastrous. To begin with, the preacher needs to be prepared in terms of his or her own stewardship and tithing commitments. The old saying is still true: "You can't teach what you don't know, and you can't lead where you won't go." No shepherd ought ever ask a flock to do what the shepherd is not willing to do himself or herself. Only a tither can beget another tither. Only a tither can testify about the verifiable truth of the Scriptures regarding tithing and tithers. Only a tither can confirm, "I know how God will make ways when you tithe. I know that God will honor his Word and bless you in ways that you cannot imagine when you tithe. I know that God is not slack concerning his promises when it comes to the tither. I am not talking about what I read or heard; I am talking about what I know from experience." Thus no one should teach or preach tithing who is not a practicing tither.

Whenever I have preached or taught tithing, I have been confronted by the Word of God to examine my own stewardship commitments to see if I am doing what I should be doing and giving as I should. Examination of one's own personal stewardship commitments is not simply a matter of calculating dollars and cents; it is also a matter of laying oneself before the Lord in one's prayer closet. The preacher's preparation begins with the practice of tithing

an excessis that leads to
/ growth

and with prayer. Tithing is not a way of raising money. It is essentially a spiritual discipline. Foundational and essential to Christian spirituality are the Word of God and prayer, or prayer and the Word of God—not either/or but both/and.

The preacher prays regarding his or her own stewardship commitments. Prayer is necessary so that the preacher will have the necessary spiritual fortitude to battle the opposition—the principalities and powers—that will seek to impede the growth in grace and discipleship that the people of God will experience when they grow in their stewardship commitments. The preacher must pray for the courage of his or her convictions and proclaim biblically based stewardship "in season and out of season"—when it is well received and when it is not, even by powerful and influential church pillars.

The preacher must pray for the ability to explain tithing properly and proclaim it powerfully, that the flock of Christ might learn and grow in the grace of giving. The preacher must pray for the Holy Spirit's guidance to say the right word at the right time with the right spirit, so that those who hear might come to understand and believe and then be persuaded to try tithing as a way of life. The preacher must pray that the Lord will bless his or her efforts and that, in spite of imperfect—and sometimes bumbling and fumbling—efforts, in spite of the human instruments and spokespersons involved, God will still get the victory, and new tithers will be won for the Kingdom.

This "preparation in the closet"—one's devotional life—involves not only prayer but also study, beginning with the Word of God. The Bible is the primary reference for tithing. Stewardship and tithing are not denominational initiatives or local church initiatives or the programmatic emphasis of a particular administration. They are the teachings of God. Before the preacher goes before the people of God, he or she must be grounded in the Word of God. Not being grounded in the Word of God on any issue about which one would speak ex cathedra is disgraceful; not being grounded in the Word of God regarding tithing is disastrous. As Paul understood that he preached not himself but a crucified, resurrected, and glorified Christ, so those individuals who would teach and proclaim tithing must understand that they present not themselves but the Word of God.

Study for leading others to tithe involves not only the Bible but the word of God that comes to us through other sources. There are a number of secondary resources, such as this one, that can help the preacher clarify his or her own positions regarding some of the issues related to tithing. Such sources can also be of assistance in preparing to address the questions of others regarding tithing. The person who is committed to tithing must remember that all questions about tithing are not hostile. Sometimes when an individual has reached closure about something and is thoroughly committed to it, one can be defensive and impatient with others who are hesitant about making commitments or who have a plethora of what seem to be elementary, "foot-dragging" questions. Teaching and preaching are definitely not for the impatient. They should be done only by committed persons who have a "shepherd's heart" and are willing to take the time to nurture and help others grow in new realms of discipleship.

There will be a number of questions of clarification regarding tithing. After all, the subject is something that is close to most Christians' hearts—money, or to be more specific, the money for which they have worked and saved and see as their own. People will have such questions as: Do you tithe off of gross or net income? Isn't tithing an Old Testament practice? What then is its meaning for those of us who are under grace and not under law? What do Jesus and the New Testament teach about tithing? What is the difference between tithing and proportionate giving? If I tithe, does that exempt me from all the other church appeals and obligations? Secondary sources will be helpful as the preacher prepares to answer both legitimate and hostile questions from those who are invited to tithe according to the Scriptures.

Facing the Congregation

After preparation comes facing the congregation. Tithing, like any other subject or idea that has the potential for radically revolutionizing a church, should not be dumped on a congregation without some prior preparation. Persons in leadership should spend time in conversation with select members of the congregation prior to the initial major presentation before the entire church. These conversations may be informal in nature and may be held with individuals, as well as taking the form of casual or teaching discussions within the context of a board or auxiliary meeting. Several things can be accomplished by these conversations and discussions. First, the preacher will have a "plausibility structure" or support group for tithing. Before any major initiative is publicly announced or presented, even if it is a revelation of the Holy Spirit, one should always have one's "troops" lined up. In any congregation or organization, there will always be those who are prepared to follow leadership if leadership lets them know what is coming and what is expected. Quarterbacks cannot expect their team members to catch a pass if those team members do not know that the ball is coming.

Secondly, prior conversations and discussions will give the preacher an indication of the kinds of questions and issues that will be raised. Thirdly, leadership may also receive some indication of the places from which opposition, or at least a chilly reception or a less-than-enthusiastic response, will come. Being forewarned ought to lead to better preparation.

Two questions that invariably arise when preparing for a major discipleship, nurture, and growth initiative on stewardship of the tithe are *when* and *how*. When do I start? How do I do it? Our answer to both questions is the same—and is simple, direct, and profound: when the Holy Spirit says so. One of the revelations that the person who spends serious time in the prayer closet (which also involves study) will receive is when and how to begin. In stewardship and tithing, as in other aspects of the work of the Kingdom, we are colaborers with Christ. The Holy Spirit works with us in preparing the soil for the seed. The Holy Spirit sets the timetable. The tithing initiative proceeds under and at the direction of the Holy Spirit. How will we know when to begin? If we have made the proper preparation in our prayer closets, we will know the acceptable time.

The Holy Spirit will also help us answer the how-to-do-it question. Stewardship and tithing methodology will vary from congregation to congregation, community to community, and leader to leader. What works in one setting will not necessarily work in another setting. What one leader with certain experiences, personality, style, or tenure is able to do may not work for another. However, the leader can take comfort in the fact that the Holy Spirit gives not only general guidelines and principles and eternal truths that are applicable for all times. The Holy Spirit also gives specific answers to specific questions from specific individuals in specific contexts to address the specific needs of specific situations.

After the leader has prepared through prayer and study and has a vanguard of believers who are ready to respond positively, the tithing message is then proclaimed with power and authority. The power comes from the Holy Spirit, and the authority comes from the Word of God. The point cannot be overly stressed that tithing has to be more than the pastor's idea, or a local church initiative, or a denominational emphasis; *tithing is the word of God.* Tithing is scripturally mandated, and those who do not tithe are robbing God, according to the Scriptures. Persons who do not tithe are disobeying God's Word, according to Malachi 3:8-10. When tithing is preached or taught in earnest, the objection is often heard, "I get so tired of hearing all of this talk about money. I don't come to church to hear about money. I come to hear the word of God." Tithing *is* the word of God. Those who proclaim God's word on tithing must do it with as much conviction as they proclaim that "Jesus saves." The latter proclamation is God's word to us about our salvation; the former proclamation is God's word to us about the beginning of our stewardship. If one is not apologetic about proclaiming that "God so loved the world," then one ought not be apologetic about pro- claiming, "Bring the full tithes." The first proclamation is about what God has already done for us; the next is about our minimum material and tangible response to God's unspeakable gift.

Tithing is not about money. Tithing is about obedience to God's Word. Tithing is about thanksgiving for what God has already done in the living and incarnate Word. Tithing is about faith in the faithfulness of God and in the written and revealed Word of God. To preach and to teach tithing is to proclaim the gospel because the gospel is about giving. Consequently, the tithing witness is also inherently, intuitively, and should be intentionally and essentially evangelistic in its thrust. The tithing witness not only strengthens saints who are already in the household of faith but also appeals to souls who are "out of the ark of safety" to give themselves to a giving God. One of the joys of my personal experience as a pastor has been receiving persons into the church through stewardship sermons. In my own experience, some of my best evangelistic preaching has been stewardship preaching.

After tithing is proclaimed through the power of the Holy Spirit and by the authority of the Word of God, how is the transition made from celebration to affirmation? In other words, how are people moved from hearing the Word to heeding the Word, that is, to becoming tithers? My own experience has been that after the Word is proclaimed, people need some tangible way to make a commitment to actually become tithers. They need to respond concretely to the proclaimed Word. The specific response may vary from church to church. Churches who have an "invitation to Christian discipleship" as part of the worship experience may call for persons to commit themselves to tithing immediately after the invitation for new members has been extended. Persons who intend to commit themselves to tithing as a way of life may be asked to stand, or sign a pledge card, or approach the altar to receive a prayer of consecration.

Earlier in this chapter, I pointed out some of the initial difficulty and disappointments I encountered when I first began to preach and teach tithing in earnest, under the direction of and with the unction of the Holy Spirit. A preacher's inclination toward hyperbole may have caused me to overstate the point. What I was attempting to show was that stewardship and tithing are not the easiest subjects to proclaim; sometimes the response may not measure up to our expectations. However, the integrity of the craft also mandates that I emphasize not only the difficulties and disappointments but also the joys and rewards of proclaiming tithing as the word of God. I would not be writing this book if those whom I try to pastor had not responded in the positive and encouraging ways that they have. The joy of proclaiming and teaching tithing has been to observe growth in grace, commitment, and spirituality in the lives of the many individuals who have entrusted their resources to a resourceful God. The joy is in hearing their marvelous stories of the many ways that the windows of heaven have been opened and God has poured on them an overflowing blessing. The joy of proclaiming tithing has been to see how God honors his Word over and over and over again. When the people of God repeatedly come up to you bubbling with joy unspeakable and say, "Reverend, it works! Tithing really works!" then you understand in a new way what Paul was talking about when he wrote to the Galatian church, "So let us not grow weary in doing what is right, for we will reap at harvest-time, if we do not give up" (Galatians 6:9, NRSV).

My hope and prayer is that the messages in this book will be of assistance to those who have the awesome and yet challenging responsibility of proclaiming to the people of God the Word of the Lord to "bring the full tithe into the storehouse, so that there may be food in my house, and thus put me to the test . . . ; see if I will not open the windows of heaven for you and pour down for you an overflowing blessing" (Malachi 3:10, NRSV).

2. You Can't Beat God Giving

Genesis 14:17-20 records the first act of tithing in the Scriptures. The text is the record not of the first sacrifice or offering or gift but of the first act of tithing in the Bible. The story behind this act of giving is an interesting one. When Abram received God's call to leave where he was and relocate to a place that God would reveal to him, Abram invited his nephew, Lot, to journey with him. Lot accepted Abram's offer and, because of his willingness to follow Abram as Abram followed the word of God, Lot was blessed materially along with Abram. The two of them were so abundantly blessed with livestock that the land on which they had settled was unable to provide for their flocks and herds. Thus strife soon developed between the herdsmen of Abram and Lot over pastures and watering holes.

Abram chose not to live in strife and confusion. No matter how much one has materially, if one has to live in strife and confusion, arguing and misunderstanding, one can still be miserable and unhappy. Strife and confusion, arguing and misunderstanding can prevent us from enjoying the blessings of God. Many persons who have much look back on times of leanness and sacrifice as "the good old days" because that was a period of less strife and confusion, arguing and misunderstanding.

Abram, as the bigger person of the two, approached his nephew and said: "Let there be no strife between you and me, between your herdsmen and my herdsmen; for we are kinsmen. Is not the whole land before you? Separate yourself from me. If you take the left hand, then I will go to the right; or if you take the right hand, then I will go to the left" (Genesis 13:8-9). When Lot surveyed the land

10

that was before him, that which was on his left was obviously more preferable to the eye. The land on the left was fertile and well watered, while the land on the right was more sparsely vegetated and barren. Instead of deferring to his uncle, by whose invitation he had been blessed, the selfish and greedy Lot chose what appeared to be the best land, leaving Abram to settle in the less desirable portion.

Lot, however, soon discovered that everything that appears to be the best at first glance is not the best in the long run. The wicked cities of Sodom and Gomorrah were in the valley chosen by Lot. Thus, he and his family lived not only in the midst of more strife and confusion, but at that time the cities of Sodom and Gomorrah, as well as the whole beautiful Jordan valley, were under the rule of a mighty warlord by the name of Chedorlaomer. In time Sodom and Gomorrah, along with several other vassal cities that were also being oppressed by Chedorlaomer, rebelled against his rule. Chedorlaomer aligned himself with several other kings, put down the rebellion, and carried off into captivity a number of the citizens of Sodom and Gomorrah, along with their possessions.

Among those who were captured was Lot. We do not know how involved Lot was in the political life of Sodom, and we do not know if he participated in the rebellion. However, since he left Abram to pitch his tent among the Sodomites, he shared in their fate. As one shares in the rewards of faith when one associates with the faithful, one also must share the punishment of sin and rebellion when one associates with the wicked.

The oaks of Mamre, the place where Abram dwelt, were less preferable than the fertile valley where Lot lived, but at least Abram was at peace there. The place where Abram dwelt was not as glamorous as Sodom, but at least Abram was free there. He was free from the political entanglements of Sodom, from the wickedness of Gomorrah, and from the rule of Chedorlaomer. The agricultural and property values of the place where Abram dwelt were not as great as the land chosen by Lot. But the blessing of God was upon the place where Abram was, and the promise of God had been given that there was a brighter day ahead. Sodom and Gomorrah have long ceased to be, but the place where Abram dwelt is still regarded as holy ground.

Word reached Abram that his nephew had been captured. Lot's

abundant possessions, which had caused the strife between him and his uncle and had led to their separation, now belonged to another as the spoils of war. Abram could have rightly said, "He made his bed; let him lie in it." Abram could have rightly said, "He chose the best part and left me the worst, no better for him." Abram could have said, "He's grown and on his own; he left my household; he's not my responsibility anymore." Or he could have said, "I would like to help him, but I am no match for Chedorlaomer. Do you expect me to risk my life and all that I have for the likes of Lot?" Abram, however, exhibited none of the understandably human attitudes of justifiable resentment that can emerge when one has been treated unfairly. Instead, he picked 318 trained men who had been born in his household, among his servants, and armed them for battle.

The fact that Abram had 318 men at his disposal, and his ability to arm them for battle, indicates that even though he dwelt in a less desirable place, God was still abundantly blessing him. Even though Abram had received the short end of the deal with Lot, heaven had made him a winner and had more than compensated him for the ingratitude of Lot. So don't worry about people who try to take advantage of your kindness. Don't worry about those who seem to get ahead at your expense. Keep on being nice. Keep on being faithful. Keep on treating people right. God will take care of you as well as those who have wronged you.

After Abram armed the men of his own household, he enlisted the support of several allies and went in pursuit of Chedorlaomer. When he came to the place where they were, Abram divided his forces, attacked by night, and routed the enemy. As Abram returned in victory from battle, he was greeted by two kings: the king of Sodom, and another whose name was Melchizedek. Melchizedek was the king of Salem, which means "peace." Salem was believed to be the ancient site or name of the city that in later times came to be known as Jerusalem, the Holy City. Melchizedek was also said to be a priest of the Most High God, and as such he and Abram shared the same faith. On his return from battle, Abram was met by the king of Sodom, for whom he had interceded, and the king of Salem, who as a priest interceded for others.

Melchizedek brought bread and wine, the chief products of the land, as symbols to express gratitude to Abram, who had brought peace, freedom, and prosperity to the land. Melchizedek blessed

Abram with the words, "Blessed be Abram by God Most High, maker of heaven and earth; and blessed be God Most High, who has delivered your enemies into your hand!" (Genesis 14:19-20). As a response to the blessings of God—as an act of thanksgiving, praise, and worship—Abram tithed, that is, gave a tenth of everything he had.

Let us note several points about this first example of tithing in the Scriptures. First, it took place at a basically early stage in the development of Abram's faith. At this point in his faith journey, Abram's name had not even been changed by God to Abraham. At this point Ishmael had not been born to Hagar, and Isaac had not been born to Sarah. At the point at which Abram first tithed, circumcision had not been given as the sign of the covenant. Sodom and Gomorrah had not yet been destroyed by God's judgment. Thus tithing was one of the early experiences in Abram's developing relationship with God.

Let us not forget that we are never too young or too new to the faith to tithe. One may have to be of a certain age to vote in church matters, but one is not too young to tithe. The smallest children can tithe; the smallest children can give to the Lord at least a tenth of whatever they have. Whether one is talking about an allowance or pocket change, the smallest child can give to the Lord a fair, proportionate amount of what he or she has. We may have to belong to a church for a certain amount of time to hold certain offices. We may feel that we need to belong to the church for a certain amount of time before we can begin to feel at home or like we really belong. But we can tithe right away. Like Abram, we need to start immediately giving to the Lord the right and proper proportion from what we have. According to God's Word, that proportion is at least 10 percent.

Secondly, we refer to Abram as "the father of faith," but as the first person to tithe in the Bible, he was also the father of tithing. Moses, the giver of the law, was not the first to tithe. The prophets were not the first to tithe. Abram, the father of faith, was the first. Thus from the outset tithing and faith are linked together in Scripture. We tithe not because it is written in the law but as an expression of our faith. No one commanded Abram to tithe; his was a voluntary gift of faith and thanksgiving. Thus when we talk about tithing, we're not simply talking about money; we're also talking about what it means to be faithful. Being faithful is more than a matter of keeping one's word and standing with the church and the Lord when things get rough. Faithfulness is more than being dutiful and diligent in exercising our responsibility. Faithfulness is also rendering unto the Lord a fair and proper proportion of all that we have. For where our treasures are, there will our hearts be also (see Matthew 6:21).

Third, the fact that Abram tithed means that tithing is of ancient origin. Tithing is no new doctrine; it may be a new concept for many of us, but it is not a new practice. It is no gimmick thought up by the church or anyone else to raise money. Tithing goes back not only to the very beginning of our faith but to the very dawn of organized and systematic religious practice. Abram was the first person to tithe in the biblical record, but he was not the first person to tithe in history. Tithing, or the giving of a sacred tenth, was practiced by a number of ancient peoples. Soon after humans began to feel the religious impulse stirring their spirits and beating within their hearts, soon after they started calling upon the name of the Lord in prayer and praise, they also started bringing expressions of thanksgiving and faith to God. At a time so far back in history that no one can identify, men and women started setting aside a minimum of 10 percent of everything they had for God.

Fourth, Abram tithed out of thanksgiving because God had blessed him with victory in battle. The blessings preceded the tithing. Abram was able to tithe because God had blessed him with something to tithe from. Let us not forget that our giving is at best a response to the fact that God has already given to us. If God had not already given, we wouldn't have anything to give. We talk about how much we give and how often we give, forgetting that God is the first and greatest giver. God is not some oppressive warlord who takes tribute money from his subjects. God is not some colonial power who exploits and robs people of that which is theirs to fill the heavenly coffers. God is a gracious heavenly Parent who has given and sacrificed for us. The verse of Scripture that some consider to be the greatest in the Bible doesn't lift up God's power, justice, majesty, holiness, and righteousness but rather God's gift to us: "For God so loved the world that he gave his only Son, that whoever believes in him should not perish but have eternal life" (John 3:16).

God never asks anything of human beings until they have first been blessed and given more than they can ever repay. The Ten Commandments begin with the words, "I am the LORD your God, who brought you out of the land of Egypt, out of the house of bondage" (Exodus 20:2). It is only after God says these words that God asks obedience from the children of Israel. God's requests are always based on his right to ask because God is the first and greatest giver.

Thus, I repeat, our giving is a response; we give because we have received. This doesn't mean that we are trying to pay God back or buy God's favor. It means that our giving begins in gratitude. We have been blessed, and so we give in thankfulness. The story is told of a man of modest means who was known for his generosity. Someone asked him why he gave so much and if he was worried about going broke. He replied, "No, not at all. I shovel out and God shovels in, and God uses a bigger shovel than I do. And God started the shoveling first."

Let us never forget that we can't beat God giving. The shovel of God, who owns the cattle on a thousand hills and all this universe's valued jewels, is bigger than ours. The shovel of God, whose pleasure it is to give us the Kingdom, is bigger than ours. The shovel of God, who is able to supply all our needs according to his riches in glory, is bigger than ours. The shovel of God, whose Word has told us to ask and we would receive, to seek and we would find, to knock and doors would be opened to us, is bigger than ours. The shovel that is bigger than ours belongs to the God who said, "Bring the full tithes into the storehouse, that there may be food in my house; and thereby put me to the test . . . if I will not open the windows of heaven for you and pour down for you an overflowing blessing" (Malachi 3:10).

The shovel of God, who made salvation available, is bigger than ours. On Calvary God gave his Son. Abram may have given a tenth, but on Calvary God gave all. I'm aware that people say, "When I come to church, I don't want to hear about money and giving. I just want to hear the gospel." But one can't really talk about the gospel without talking about giving because at the heart of the gospel is a God who gives. And because God gives first, we too ought to give in thanksgiving.

I know that some of us get weary of giving and tired of hearing pleas and sermons about giving. Sometimes we wonder if we will ever reach a point where we can stop giving. Well, when God stops giving to us, we can stop giving. When God stops making ways out of no ways for us, we can stop giving. When God stops being our company keeper when we're lonely and stops helping us pull together the broken pieces of our lives when loved ones are taken from us, we can stop giving. When God stops giving us grace sufficient to match our trials, strength to bear our crosses, and courage to face our tomorrows, we can stop giving. When God stops putting food on our table, helping us raise children, and providing for our families, we can stop giving. When the blood given by Jesus no longer avails for our sins, when the eternal flow of God's love is dried up and we're left alone against "the wiles of the devil," when the Holy Spirit refuses to give up power for us to be victorious in life and death, then we can stop giving. But as long as God gives, we also ought gladly give, and that's all right because

> You can't beat God giving, no matter how you try,
> And just as sure as you are living and the Lord is in heaven on
> high,
> The more you give, the more God gives to you.
> But keep on giving Because it's really true that
> you can't beat God giving, no matter how you try.
> Should we receive and never give?
> The Savior died that we might live.
> His life on Calvary He gladly gave,
> Our sinful souls to save.[1]

1. "You Can't Beat God Giving" by Doris Akers. © Copyright 1957 by Manna Music, Inc., 35255 Brooten Road, Pacific City, OR 97135. All rights reserved. Used by permission.

3. Let's Go Back to Bethel

Genesis 28:18-22 and Genesis 35:1-3

It must have been one of the loneliest nights of his life. Jacob, his youngest son, had run away from home. As he faced the reality of his failing strength and eyesight, Isaac found himself thinking more and more about the inevitability of death with each passing day. Isaac recognized that part of the preparation for his home-going involved passing the mantle of family leadership and making disposition of his estate between his two sons.

Esau, the eldest, had certain rights of inheritance that were inherent in his being the oldest. Isaac consequently prepared to bless Esau as head of the family and as the one who would receive the larger portion of the inheritance. However, Isaac's wife, Rebekah, favored their son Jacob over Esau and successfully conspired with him to steal his elder brother's blessing. When Esau discovered that his younger brother had cheated him out of both his birthright and his blessing, he swore that Jacob would not live to enjoy the rewards of his trickery.

No matter what we're after, the way we get it is just as important as getting it. If we don't pursue our goals in the right way, we might not be able to enjoy them after we have attained them. Esau recognized that although there was nothing he could do about his lost birthright and stolen blessing, he could do something to prevent Jacob from enjoying what rightfully belonged to his brother. Esau resolved that when his father died he would kill Jacob. Rebekah learned of Esau's designs and told Jacob to run fast and far to the distant home of her brother, Laban, to flee the wrath of his elder brother, and to stay away until Esau's anger had abated.

In our text we find Jacob by himself in the middle of the night,

17

exiled from home, fleeing the murderous wrath of his brother. There he was, miles from his home in Beersheba, perhaps on the first long journey of his life. The journey from home, from the familiar, to new adventures, new ideas, new places, and new persons is always a long and difficult journey to make. There he was, the grandson of Abraham, father of the faith; there he was, the son of Isaac, whose own life had been spared because of his father's faith; there he was, separated from all that he knew and loved. There he was, on the bleak summit of the Bethel plateau, with his head propped upon a stone for a pillow, looking above him at the starlit sky. There he lay, feet sore, body tired, eyes heavy, mind anxious about his future, heart burdened, and spirit depressed.

Out there by himself, Jacob discovered he was not alone. Out there, while feeling dejected, he discovered that he was not deserted. Out there, away from the reach of Esau, Jacob discovered that he was not out of the reach of God. As Jacob dreamed, he saw the vision of a ladder or stairway that stretched from heaven to earth upon which angels were ascending and descending. The Lord who stood above it told Jacob that one day his descendants would dwell in the land and in the place where he slept. Jacob received the further assurance that God would be with him wherever he went and would one day bring him back to the land and place where he presently was. Jacob awoke and said: "Surely the LORD is in this place and I did not know it! . . . How awesome is this place! This is none other than the house of God, and this is the gate of heaven" (Genesis 28:16-17, NRSV).

The next morning Jacob took the stone that had been his pillow and set it up as a pillar, a monument, and consecrated it by pouring oil on it. He called the place Bethel, which means "house of God." There Jacob made a vow, saying, "If God will be with me, and will keep me in this way that I go, and will give me bread to eat and clothing to wear, so that I come again to my father's house in peace, then the LORD shall be my God, and this stone, which I have set up for a pillar, shall be God's house; and of all that you give me I will surely give one tenth to you" (Genesis 28:20-22, NRSV).

Let us note a couple of things about Jacob's pledge to tithe. First, Jacob's pledge was made when he was a wandering fugitive from his parent's home in search of another place to call home. His pledge was made when he was at his weakest financially, when he didn't have much of anything, when he could least afford it. His pledge was based on his faith that God would provide him the means to keep his pledge.

We ought never assume that persons who tithe are necessarily more prosperous and free of debt than others. We ought never assume that those who pledge to tithe know for sure that they will be able to keep their pledge or that they know how they will pay their tithe. I would guess that a number of people who pledge to tithe are not sure that they will be able to afford to tithe. We ought never assume that persons who tithe have their financial situation all worked out. "If they had my bills, they wouldn't be tithing," some might say. How do you know they don't have as many bills as you? Maybe if you had their faith, you would be tithing also! Many of us pledge when we can least afford to do so. Like Jacob, many persons who pledge to tithe are financially shaky at best. Jacob's pledge was a result of his belief in God's promise of protection and care for him. Most persons I know pledge on the same basis. We pledge in faith that God will help us and provide the means for us to keep our pledge. We pledge on the promise of God that we will be cared for and provided for. I repeat: to pledge is to make a faith commitment, and "faith is the substance of things hoped for" (Hebrews 11:1, KJV). The apostle Paul reminds us, ". . . in hope we were saved. Now hope that is seen is not hope. For who hopes for what is seen? But if we hope for what we do not see, we wait for it with patience" (Romans 8:24-25, NRSV).

Secondly, Jacob's pledge to tithe was a voluntary act. Jacob did not tithe because tithing was part of God's law at that time. Those who correctly observe that tithing later became part of the Old Testament law might then ask, "Since we are under the new dispensation of grace, does the Old Testament law of the tithe apply to us?" Let us note that the first Old Testament tithers were persons who were not under the law. The first Old Testament tither was Abraham. In Genesis 14:20 Abraham tithed to Melchizedek a tenth of everything he had (not of his net but of his gross) as an act of thanksgiving to God for victory in a battle. In Genesis 28 Jacob pledged to tithe to God a tenth of all he had. Both of these incidents occurred many generations before the law was given to Moses. Thus even in the Old Testament the first instances of tithing were expressions of thanksgiving and faith, not law.

We tithe because the Scriptures identify tithing as an appropriate standard, one way of expressing thanksgiving and faith. Other standards of giving lifted up by the Scriptures, particularly the New Testament, include that of the widow, who gave the two mites; Barnabas, who sold his field and brought the money and laid it at the apostles' feet; and Jesus, who gave his life. Each gave not a tenth but all. Their gifts of all, like Abraham's and Jacob's gift of the tenth, were given voluntarily, as acts of thanksgiving and expressions of faith. Let us never forget that tithing is giving, and giving is at its best when it is done not grudgingly nor out of a sense of necessity, but voluntarily. For "God loves a cheerful giver" (2 Corinthians 9:7, NRSV). God has given us so much and been so good to us that we cheerfully give back what God asks.

At the close of Genesis 28, we see Jacob, the homeless young man, making a faith pledge to give God a tenth. By the opening of chapter 35, over thirty years have passed. We can observe two things. First, God has kept the promise made at Bethel; second, Jacob has not. Since the time that Jacob as a young man rested his head on the stone in the middle of the night, he had become a very wealthy and powerful person in the region where he lived. He had settled at Shechem with his large family of twelve sons and one daughter. He owned herds of livestock, and his land holdings were vast. God had truly been good to Jacob and had kept every promise made to him. Jacob, however, had evidently become so comfortable at Shechem that he had forgotten about the vow he had made at Bethel when God had come to him at midnight and spoke peace to his troubled spirit. He had forgotten his promise to return to the spot of his heavenly visitation and build an altar there. He had forgotten that he had promised to give a tenth of all he had to God.

It's easy to become so comfortable and accustomed to the good life at Shechem that we forget about the promises we made at Bethel. That's why I believe that every now and then we ought to rededicate ourselves anew to God. That's why I believe in renewing our stewardship and reviewing our discipleship commitments. It's easy to forget the promises we made when we were scared and desperate, when we were humble and thankful, or when we first felt the presence of Christ and the power of the Holy Spirit.

But though our memories are short, God's memory is long. God came to Jacob and told him, "Arise, go up to Bethel, and dwell there; and make there an altar to the God who appeared to you when you fled from your brother Esau" (Genesis 35:1). Jacob then went to his household and said: "Put away the foreign gods that are among you, and purify yourselves, and change your garments; then let us arise and go up to Bethel, that I may make there an altar to the God who answered me in the day of my distress and has been with me wherever I have gone" (Genesis 35:2-3). Not only had Jacob forgotten his vow, but he had allowed strange gods to infiltrate his household. When we forget our word to God and God's word to us, it's easy to become infiltrated by strange gods, strange doctrines, and strange ideas. When we fail to do as we promised, when we disregard our vows, it's easy to adopt strange ways and habits that are foreign to our background. When we fail to remember the God of Bethel, when we fail to worship the God who picked us up when we had nothing in the day of our distress, it's easy to start making allowances and compromises and permitting things that we know we shouldn't. Forgotten vows to our forgotten God at a forgotten Bethel lead to strange gods and strange ways. Incorrect and forgotten stewardship commitments lead to shady discipleship. When we fail to give to God as we ought, we start spending our money in strange ways on strange things, buying what we wouldn't buy otherwise. When we fail to keep God first in our giving, God also ceases to be first in our living.

Maybe that's why the spiritual life of the church is sometimes so poor, and our stewardship has become so shaky. When the early church had needs, people sacrificed and gave as God had prospered them. They didn't give what they didn't have; they gave as God had given to them. Somewhere we started believing that we needed to get something back for what we gave other than the blessings that God has given and continues to give. We started pushing tickets, pushing tapes, and pushing shows. More sins and strange practices have entered the life of the church through some of our fund-raising. Some of us are going to end up in hell over the things we do under the banner of raising money for the church. We—all of us—preachers, officers, church members—have allowed all kinds of strange practices to enter the household of faith. God's Word comes to us and tells us to put away these foreign practices that are damning the souls and ruining the spirit in the church. Stop selling some of these strange things that we wouldn't want the Lord to catch us buying or doing. Put away some of these strange trips to some of the strange places we wouldn't want the Lord to catch us going to. The Lord knows what we are doing in his church's name. Let's go back to the Bethel of sound biblical giving and stewardship where we pledge: "I'll erect an altar in my heart and give at least a tenth of all you give to me."

We need not only to return to our Bethels of biblical stewardship and tithing; we need to return to other Bethels of broken promises and forgotten vows. Some of us who are walking around healthy, mean, and cantankerous need to remember how we promised the Lord on a sickbed that if he healed us we'd turn over a new leaf and be a better person. We need to go back to that Bethel and do as we promised. Some of us as mature Christians who have become too comfortable in our Shechems need to remember the Bethels of our home training. We were taught to give in the church and to the church with thanksgiving and faith. We were taught to respect God's church, God's preacher, and God's people. We were taught to be kind and not to talk about people or look down on people less fortunate than we. We need to remember what others taught us and what we promised them before they went home to glory. Maybe, like Jacob, we were wandering around lost in life, confused and lonely, but the grace of God found us and comforted us in the day of our distress. We made a decision to live for Jesus, but since that time we've allowed Satan to steal our joy. We need to find our way back to Bethel. Some of us as leaders—as preachers and officers, presidents and persons with influence—have forgotten that we hold our positions to serve, not to be served; to give, not to be given; to do God's will, not push our own program; to act in the best interest of the church and not the best interest of our egos or power. We need to go back to Bethel.

When Jacob went back to Bethel, God met him there and called him again by his new name, Israel, given to him at the Jabbok, and repeated the promise made in times past. When we return to Bethel, God will meet us there. We'll hear God speak afresh, hear God's word in a new way, and receive a new vision and a new name. Like the hymn writer, we need to ask:

Where is the blessedness I knew, When first I saw the Lord?
Where is the soul-refreshing view of Jesus and His word?
What peaceful hours I then enjoyed, How sweet their memory
still!
But they have left on aching void The world can never fill.
Return, O Holy Dove, return, Sweet Messenger of rest!
I hate the sins that made Thee mourn, And drove Thee from
my breast.
So shall my walk be close with God, Calm and serene my
frame;
So purer light shall mark the road That leads me to the Lamb.[1]

1. William Cowper, "O for a Closer Walk with God."

4. Will Anyone Rob God?

Malachi 3:8

A true perception of who and what we are, a proper attitude toward all that we have, and a correct approach to giving are dependent on our acceptance of one central truth. This particular truth is a surprise to some of us, a bitter pill for others of us to swallow, and totally unacceptable to still others of us. Lest we forget, however, truth does not depend on our acceptance to be truth. Sometimes when we hear certain truths of our faith declared or expounded, we say, "I don't believe that" or "I disagree with that." But truth is truth whether or not we like it, believe it, or accept it. Truth is not decided by popular consensus or majority vote, by individual opinion or personal preference. Truth is truth all by itself.

For example, we cannot decree God out of existence by simply declaring that God doesn't exist or by saying we don't believe in God. God is the central integrating, ontological truth of the universe, and God exists whether we believe in God or not. God is real, God's word is true, God's promises are sure, God's power is real, whether we accept them or not. When we say that God doesn't exist, we only exemplify the ancient truth expressed by the psalmist when he declared, "The fool says in his heart, 'There is no God' " (Psalm 14:1). God is not dependent on us for God's existence, but we are surely dependent on God for ours.

The difficult truth we must accept if we are to have a right understanding of who and what we are, a proper attitude toward all that we possess, and a correct approach to giving is this: God is the owner of everything, and we are the owners of nothing. That's a hard truth to hear as well as to accept. Right now someone is thinking, "Preacher, let me make sure I'm really hearing what I think

24

I'm hearing before I finish tuning you out—or prepare to take a nap. Are you telling me that I do not actually own the car I drive with my name on the title, those monogrammed clothes I wear, my favorite jewelry, the house with my name on the mortgage or deed, or the money in the bank with my name on the account? Are you telling me that I don't own these things when I've worked hard for everything I have? Nobody gave me anything! How dare you tell me that I don't own what I possess, not after I've been going to work faithfully these many years—battling inclement weather and fighting traffic; dealing with hardheaded and difficult coworkers; toiling long and hard for unappreciative bosses, companies, and constituencies; being paid less than I deserve so that I can purchase what I have. And now you are telling me that I don't own it? Preacher, give me a break!"

Yes, that's exactly the truth that I bring to you. We work hard for the privilege of possessing some things in this life and using some things for our enjoyment or to make life easier. Possession, however, and the privileges of use and enjoyment do not constitute ownership. The stars are ours to behold, but we don't own them. The warmth of the sun is ours to feel, but we don't own it. Music is ours to hear, but we don't own it. Love is ours to be fulfilled, but we don't own love. We may have a companion, wife, husband, children, or friends, but we don't own them. The trouble with so many relationships is that sometimes we forget that we don't own people. God is against all kinds of slavery, whether it's racial slavery, political slavery, economic slavery, social slavery, family slavery, love slavery, church slavery, or the slavery of sin. God doesn't give us loved ones and companions, friends and children, for us to do with as we please; we don't own anyone.

We don't even own ourselves. We cannot wake ourselves up in the morning. We cannot determine our health. We cannot stop ourselves from aging. We cannot stop death from coming. We cannot even make ourselves do right. Even a stalwart saint like Paul had to admit, "I can will what is right, but I cannot do it. For I do not do the good I want, but the evil I do not want is what I do" (Romans 7:18b-19).

If you believe you own the car you drive, try taking it with you when you lie down to die. If you think you own that house you've paid for or the money you've saved in the bank, try taking them with you into death. We can buy things for ourselves, but we can't take them with us. The pharaohs of Egypt thought they could take their riches with them to the next world. They built great pyramids to house their treasured possessions so that they might still enjoy them. I do not know where in the next world the pharaohs are, but the things they buried with them are scattered in museums and private collections all over the world for others to enjoy.

Even if we are buried in our car or our favorite dress or suit, even if we're wearing our favorite piece of jewelry, even if our money is placed in our casket with us, we still don't take any of it with us. Our possessions remain buried, while our souls answer to a just and righteous God. When we appear before the judgment seat of Christ, we will not be seated in a Mercedes, Lincoln, or Cadillac. We will not be wearing our treasured ring or necklace, mink coat, tailored suit, or our Bruno Magli shoes. That was the discovery of the rich fool in the parable of Luke 12. And that was the discovery of the rich man in the parable of Luke 16. Job hit the nail right on the head when he said, "Naked I came from my mother's womb, and naked shall I return; the LORD gave, and the LORD has taken away; blessed be the name of the LORD" (Job 1:21).

When we appear before the judgment and, thanks be to God, the mercy seat of Christ, we will have with us all that we truly own: our character. Our character is truly our own; we've worked for it and earned it. We cannot pass our character off to others, and others cannot pass theirs to us. Our character—what we are, not what we possess. Our character—who we really are, not who we think we are or pretend to be. Our character—our integrity and honesty, our devotion to truth and righteousness, our passion for justice, our love for others. Our character will follow us throughout eternity. When the Book of Life is opened, our bank accounts will not be examined, but our character will be weighed in the balance between the judgment and the grace of God.

On the morn of that eternal day, we will have our faith—the faith by which we've lived and the faith by which we've died; the faith through which we've praised and served God; the faith that has caused us to be a blessing to others, the faith that has inspired us to give so much, so often, for so long. We cannot bequeath our faith to others, and others cannot will their faith to us. Each of us must come to a personal and full knowledge of God for ourselves. Our experience with God, our testimonies, our depth in the Spirit are ours. Others may have similar experiences, for it is no secret what God can do, what God has done for some and will do for others. Yet no two individuals are alike, as no two lives are alike, as no two snowflakes are alike, as no two earthly pilgrimages with God are exactly alike. In my life I've had to labor with some things that you haven't, and in your life you've had some burdens that I haven't had. Each of our lives bears the marks of God's special work. That's why some of us shout, some of us cry, some of us dance, some of us laugh, and some of us just close our eyes. When we stand before God, we will stand with a faith that is uniquely ours.

Our character and our faith are about all that we truly own that will accompany us beyond the grave and into eternity. Everything else that we possess belongs to God. We manage only the blessings God gives us directly—or gives us the health, strength, and wisdom to acquire. The word that the New Testament uses to describe this management is *oikonomia*, which is translated as "stewardship." The original meaning of the word *economics* or *oikonomas* referred to more than money; it referred to the whole ordering, administration, or management of life.

This is the time for each of us to look at our life and then raise the question, "What kind of a manager am I?" How are we managing the bodies we inhabit? "Do you not know," asks 1 Corinthians 6:19-20, "that your body is a temple of the Holy Spirit within you, which you have from God? You are not your own; you were bought with a price. So glorify God in your body." How are we managing our minds? Jesus reminds us of God's command: "You shall love the Lord your God with all your heart, with all your soul, and with all your mind" (Matthew 22:37). How are we managing our time? The psalmist declared, " 'Thou art my God.' My times are in thy hand . . ." (Psalm 31:14-15). How are we managing our youth? Ecclesiastes reminds us, "Remember also your Creator in the days of your youth, before the evil days come, and the years draw nigh, when you will say, 'I have no pleasure in them' " (Ecclesiastes 12:1). How are we managing our lives? Jesus said, "Therefore do not be anxious, saying, 'What shall we eat?' or 'What shall we drink?' or 'What shall we wear?' . . . your heavenly Father knows that you need them all. But seek first his kingdom and his righteousness, and all these things shall be yours as well" (Matthew 6:31-33).

To mismanage what belongs to us is carelessness and callousness, stupidity and shortsightedness, but to mismanage what belongs to God is robbery. In addition to the other areas of life, each of us ought to raise the question, "How am I managing God's money?" The prophet Malachi, speaking for God, asks a crucial question: "Will anyone rob God? Yet you are robbing me! But you say, 'How are we robbing you?' In your tithes and offerings!" (3:8-9, NRSV). We rob by taking or withholding what belongs to another. God in his Word has asked that we return a minimum of one-tenth of all that we possess as an expression of thanksgiving. Leviticus 27:30 tells us, "All the tithe of the land, whether of the seed of the land or of the fruit of the trees, is the LORD's; it is holy to the LORD."

Will anyone rob God? A Chinese preacher once said, "It came to pass that a man went to a market with a purse of ten coins. Seeing a beggar, he gave the poor man nine of the coins and kept only one for himself. The beggar, instead of being thankful for what he had received, followed the good man and stole the tenth coin also."[1] "Will anyone rob God? Yet you are robbing me! But you say, 'How are we robbing you?' In tithes and offerings!"

Many of us feel that we ought to give God whatever we want, without any guidelines. A preacher once went to a barber who was opposed to pledging and tithing. The barber said, "I think a person should give just what he feels like giving." When the haircut was finished, the preacher gave the barber a quarter. The barber said indignantly, "Preacher, haircuts are six dollars." The preacher said, "I thought you just finished saying that we should give God just what we feel like giving him, and I know you're not better than God."[2]

We pay the electric company whatever it asks, but we give God, who gives to us the light of the sun and eyes to behold it, whatever we want. We give the phone company whatever it asks, but we give God, who gives us speech, whatever we want. We give the grocery store whatever it asks, but we give God, who makes the crops grow, whatever we want. We give the water company whatever it asks, but we give God, who sends us free rain to water lawns and fields and to supply the reservoirs, whatever we want. We give the government whatever taxes it asks, but we give God, who holds nations in the hollow of his hand, whatever we want. We go to movies, concerts, and sporting events and pay whatever admission they ask, but we come to church, where the gospel of salvation for our souls is proclaimed, and become upset if a special amount is asked for. We give the doctor whatever is charged, but we give God, who wakes us up in the morning and gives us the activity of our limbs, whatever we want. We give lawyers whatever they charge to plead our case, but we give God, whose Son Jesus died on Calvary to redeem us, whatever we want. "Will anyone rob God? Yet you are robbing me! But you say, 'How are we robbing you?' In tithes and offerings!"

We're either living by theft or we're living by trust. Some of us have been living by theft. We've been withholding from the Lord for a long time. We've been withholding praise that belongs to God, talent that belongs to God, time that belongs to God, money that belongs to God, service that belongs to God, skills and knowledge that belong to God, and a life that belongs to God—for a long time. Some of us have been living by theft for so long we're ashamed to admit our lack of faith and our failure to live and give according to the Word of the Lord. Some of us are scared to live any other way. Some of us don't believe we can live any other way.

However, I implore you by the Word and the power and the Spirit of God, not to let pride or fear or stubbornness stand in the way of the blessings, peace, and joy of a life of trust. Don't ever believe that it's too late to start living by trust. The Good News of the gospel is that if you have the desire and the will to do better, it's not too late. If the despised tax collector Zacchaeus could start living by trust when he said, "The half of my goods I give to the poor; and if I have defrauded anyone of anything, I restore it fourfold" (Luke 19:8), then it's not too late for you. If the misguided Saul on the Damascus road (Acts 9) could start living by trust when he asked, "Lord, what will you have me to do?" then it's not too late for you. If a prodigal son could come to himself in a hog pen and decide to trust the love of a compassionate father and go home, then it's not too late for you. If a dying thief could recognize the majesty of Christ even as he was stretched wide and hung high on a cross and be moved to say, "Jesus, remember me when you come into your kingdom," and if that dying thief could receive the assurance, "Today you will be with me in Paradise" (Luke 23:42-43, NRSV), then it's not too late for you.

Quit robbing God; quit withholding from God. Be honest with God, and start living by trust. Trust God to take care of you and provide for your needs. In times of crisis, trust God to make a way out of no way. In times of distress, trust God to fight your battles. In times of testing, trust God to justify your faith. In times of loneliness, trust God never to leave you. Trust God to keep his Word: "Bring the full tithe into the storehouse, so that there may be food in my house, and thus put me to the test, says the LORD of hosts; see if I will not open the windows of heaven for you and pour down for you an overflowing blessing" (Malachi 3:10, NRSV).

1. Robert C. Shannon and Michael J. Shannon, *Stewardship Source Book* (Cincinnati: Standard Publishing, 1987), 9.
2. Ibid., 80.

5. When You Care Enough to Give the Very Best

Genesis 4:1-5

Every one of us who has ever contributed anything to what we consider to be a worthy and honorable cause has asked the question, "How much shall I give?" Every one of us who has ever put anything in an offering plate has asked the question, "What shall I put in?" or "What shall I give to God and to the church?" When we really think about the questions of what and how much to give to God, we will discover that they are the most central and fundamental questions of our lives. These questions are not new questions but go back to the very dawn of creation.

The questions of what and how much to give to God were the first questions that Adam and Eve, the first man and woman created by God, had to answer. Adam and Eve were placed in the garden of Eden in a state of idyllic existence, which we refer to as Paradise, a state that was free from worry and work, sin and suffering, debt and death. God told Adam and Eve that they had free access to everything they saw and wanted, with the exception of the fruit of the tree of knowledge of good and evil. The very first question that Adam and Eve had to answer was how much obedience they were willing to give to God. They chose not to give total obedience, and dire consequences resulted—they lost Paradise! They lost that ideal easiness that we as humans have been trying to recover ever since that dreadful day when our first parents chose to give less than they should to God.

As the text indicates, the questions of what and how much should be given to God turned out to be the two major decisions that the oldest sons of Adam and Eve, whose names were Cain and Abel, had to make. Although they didn't realize it at the time, these questions were the things upon which their futures hung and their destinies turned. Cain, the elder of the two, became a farmer, while Abel became a sheep herder. In time these two young men, like their parents before them and every one of us after them, had to answer the question, "What and how much shall I give to God?" The occasion for these questions was the bringing of an offering of the work of their hands to God. Cain brought an offering of the fruit of the ground, and Abel brought the firstlings of his flock and their fat portions.

The Scriptures tell us that the Lord had regard for Abel's offering but not for Cain's. The question naturally arises of why Abel's offering was more favorably received than Cain's. As we think about this passage, we observe that each of them brought the work of their own hands. Cain did not borrow Abel's sheep, and Abel did not try to bring any of Cain's fruit. As we try to answer the questions of how much and what we should give to God, the first thing we must realize is that we can give only from the works of our own hands. God has never required us to give what we don't have or haven't produced. Sometimes some of us worry and become discouraged and frustrated because we cannot give what is asked for by the pastor or the church. We must never forget that the God to whom we are giving does not expect us to give what we truly do not have, but God does expect us to do our best with the fruit of our own hands. You may not be able to give what others give when you don't earn their salary. You may not be able to render the same kind of service that someone else renders when you don't have the same talent, youth, education, or physical ability or vitality. You cannot give sheep if you have been raising corn, and you cannot give corn if you have been raising sheep—and the Lord doesn't expect you to do so. But the Lord does expect a decent offering of the fruit that you do have. If Abel's offering was well received and Cain's was not, the reason was not that God was more appreciative of sheep than of fruit. That would have been unjust, for it would have meant that Cain would have had to bring what he didn't have. There had to have been another reason than the simple fact that Abel brought sheep and Cain brought fruit.

According to the Scriptures, "Cain brought to the LORD an

offering of the fruit of the ground, and Abel brought of the firstlings of his flock and of their fat portions" (Genesis 4:3-4). The difference between the offerings of Cain and Abel was not simply one of substance or quantity but also one of quality. The text says that Abel brought the firstlings of his flock and the fat portions thereof, but they do not say that Cain brought the first fruits and the ripest thereof but that he simply brought fruit of the ground. The fruit that Cain brought could have been what was left over after he had used all he wanted or marketed all he could. The fruit that Cain brought could have been that which was smallest or stunted in growth, or that which was going bad, or that which could not be marketed or used by him personally. Cain gave an offering without sacrifice; he gave a token without any real commitment to God. Cain gave begrudgingly rather than generously; he gave with an attitude rather than with gratitude. He gave with his hand but not with his heart.

Abel's offering, however, involved sacrifice, commitment, generosity, and a real sense of caring and sharing. Abel offered not the lean, the lame, the weakest, and the oldest of his flock, but the firstlings. Abel offered that which was highly esteemed and precious in his sight. Abel offered to God the firstlings, the best of his flock, and the fat thereof, the best of the best.

The difference between Cain and Abel is that Abel "cared enough to give his very best." Most of you will recognize this as the slogan of Hallmark, the greeting card company. Several assumptions lie behind their familiar slogan. One is that their brand of card is the best. Another is that people tend to send cards to those whom they care about. Another is that people who truly care for others want to give the best. A fourth assumption is that people who truly care for others do not mind paying or giving a little more because they want the best for those whom they care about.

No matter what the cause, project, institution, or person, we truly give our best when we care. We can give without caring, but we cannot care without giving. Sometimes our giving has little to do with caring. Sometimes we give out of a sense of obligation or duty. We give not because we want to but because we are expected to. We are committed not to the Lord but to our position or office, our job, our responsibility, and our image. Thus, we give because giving is the price that we must pay to fulfill our role. Sometimes we give out of fear. Some people give because they are afraid that if they don't give, God will cut off their blessings. Some people believe that if they don't give, they will begin to have "bad luck"—whatever that is. As Christians we don't believe in luck; we believe in God. Giving is not some holy insurance policy that we invest in as a hedge against trouble. We don't give because we are trying to keep any alleged run of "good luck" going. We don't give because we are trying to ensure God's blessings or favor. First of all, God's favor is not for sale. Secondly, even if it were for sale, we wouldn't have enough money to buy it. No, we give not because we are trying to buy God but because we love God—and love God enough to give our very best.

Sometimes we give because we expect to receive something in return. We believe that if we take care of God, then God will take care of us. We believe that if we give to God, then God will bless us. Though this is true, our primary reason for giving should not be that giving to God is a good investment that pays sizeable dividends and returns. God and the church are not business investments to sink money into for profit. Some of us give like we're playing the numbers or the lottery. We put down a minimum fifty-cent or one-dollar offering and expect God to open heaven's windows and bless us to maximum proportions. Our motivation for giving should not be a selfish desire to get back something greater than what we have given. Whether or not God blesses us in ways that we desire, we should give. We give not because of what we expect in return but because we love God, and because we love God enough to give our very best.

Abel cared enough to give the very best. He gave not only the firstlings of his flock but also the fat portions, which were considered to be choicest portions for sacrifice. Abel cared enough to give God the best of his best. He gave God sufficient of his choicest resources.

We know what to give—the best. Now we must ask ourselves how much of the best we should give. When the Bible speaks of giving, it refers to tithes and offerings. It does not mentions trips, dinners, raffles, contests, sales, or tickets, but tithes and offerings. In the Scriptures God asked people to give a minimum of 10 percent of whatever they received. *Tithe* means a tenth. Some people who give regularly therefore consider themselves to be tithers. While regular and consistent giving is good stewardship discipline, it is not necessarily tithing. Tithing means one-tenth, and unless one is giving at least one-tenth, then one is not tithing.

In the Scriptures the first 10 percent of a person's income, whatever it was and however it came, was set aside as the Lord's tithe and was considered holy. Leviticus 27:30 states, "All the tithe of the land, whether of the seed of the land or of the fruit of the trees, is the LORD's; it is holy to the LORD." Since it was believed that the 10 percent was the Lord's anyway, one did not begin to give an offering until one went beyond the 10 percent. In view of the Scriptures, therefore, the tithe was 10 percent and the minimum that an individual gave to God. The tithe was the Lord's and was set aside and looked upon as holy.

The offering was what one gave beyond the tithe. Some of us think that the tithe is the maximum and that once we have tithed, we have given all. But the tithe is not the maximum; it is the minimum. That's why the Scriptures speak of tithes and offerings. What most of us call an offering is not really an offering since most of us don't give even the basic tithe, of which the offering is but an extension.

Some will question the biblical standard of giving as stiff, tough, and demanding. The amount of money the Scriptures call for as a minimum standard for giving will be looked upon as too much by some. For others it will seem a great sacrifice. However, if we really care, then no amount is too great and no sacrifice is too large. For how can we put a price tag on love? Love can be demanding because it costs to love. Anyone who wants to get away with giving minimums does not love because whether we are loving God, a friend, our children, our spouse, our relatives, our church, or even an enemy, love calls for maximums not minimums. That's why one has to really love God to tithe with the right spirit. Tithing requires a level of cheerful giving or commitment that can be attained only through love. Instead of asking, "Can I afford to tithe?" maybe we ought to ask, "Do I love God enough to try to give the very best of myself and my treasures?"

When one gives out of a sense of duty, one says, "I give because I should give." When one gives out of fear, one says, "I give because I had better give." When one gives because one expects something in return, one says, "I give because it is appropriate to give." When one gives because one cares, one says, "I give because I want to give. I give because this person, this God, this church, this cause means something to me. What I regret is not that it's time to give or the amount that I am going to give but that I cannot give more. Because I care, I want to give my very best."

Whenever we begin to complain about what or how much God asks of us, we need to remind ourselves that God asks no more of us than God gives to us. We serve a God who gives us the best. By day God provides the sun—the best light. By night God provides the moon and stars—the best guides through the darkness. When we are thirsty, God provides the rain—the best water. When we long for the aesthetic, God provides a sunrise or a sunset—the best beauty. When we need comfort and strength, God provides the Holy Spirit—the best inspiration. And when we needed a Savior, God gave us his best—Jesus, the only begotten Son. As somebody said: God (the greatest lover) so loved (the greatest degree) the world (the greatest number) that he gave (the greatest act) his only begotten Son (the greatest gift) that whosoever (the greatest invitation) believes (the greatest simplicity) in him (the greatest person) should not perish (the greatest deliverance) but (the greatest difference) have (the greatest certainty) everlasting life (the greatest possession).

God gave us not only his best but, in Jesus, the best of his best. Can we, dare we, do any less than give back to God the best of our best?

6. When You Care Enough to Give Your All

Mark 12:41-44

It had been a draining afternoon in the temple for Jesus. The guardians of the religious status quo represented by the scribes, Pharisees, and Sadducees were becoming more and more vocal and aggressive in their opposition to the teachings and ministry of Jesus. Our Lord, knowing that his time on earth was quickly coming to a close, and realizing that there was still too much to do and say, had increased his denunciations of those who opposed his gospel. All of the niceties of polite debate and disagreement were gone—and their mutual disdain for what the other represented was evident for all to see.

Despite this tension between the Master and the hierarchy of Judaism, despite his disagreement with much of what went on in the temple, Jesus continued to go. He did not let disagreeable personalities and conflicts stop him from worshiping or serving God in the place that had been set aside as God's house. At this point in his ministry, it would have been easier for him to divorce himself from the temple and its traditions and take his message to the fields, along the shores, and in the villages and hamlets outside Jerusalem. Whenever he went to worship, there were always those who were waiting to find fault and trap him in his words. They watched everything he did and listened to everything he said, not so they could be helped thereby but so they could criticize. Nevertheless, Jesus went to the temple because he was determined that nothing and nobody would interfere with his worship of God.

On this particular day, while in the temple—while at "church," so to speak—the Pharisees had tried to trap him with a question about paying taxes, the Sadducees had tested him with a question about the resurrection, and a scribe had asked him about the first commandment. After answering them all, Jesus had warned the people about ostentatious displays of piety and about scrambling for positions and places of honor in the church. Now, as he was on his way out of the temple, he stopped in the area opposite the treasury. In the temple between the Court of Gentiles and the Court of Women was the Gate Beautiful. Jesus may have paused there to reflect and be quiet after the afternoon's confrontations, discussions, and tensions.

All of us have had periods of difficulty and discouragement, frustration and depression. And sometimes when we have been most deeply engrossed in a particular circumstance, it seems as if, from out of the blue, from a completely different source, God sends some good news or we hear from someone special or we see something that brightens our day, lifts our spirits, and refreshes and inspires us to go on. Sometimes that special word or incident isn't much, but it's just what we need at that moment to give us that little extra push to go on by faith.

As Jesus sat opposite the treasury that day, he had the same kind of experience. In the Court of Women were thirteen trumpet-shaped collection receptacles into which people cast their offerings after they had made their primary sacrifice in the temple—after they had paid their tithe, their sacred and holy tenth of their income unto the Lord. Each of these offerings was for a special purpose, such as the purchase of corn, oil, or wine for sacrifices; temple administration and maintenance; and perhaps another for the poor. Whenever a contribution was thrown into one of these trumpets, the clanging sound of metal hitting metal was heard. The larger the coins and the offerings, the louder the clang. Some people contributed generously to these extra offerings, and the trumpets announced their contributions with the appropriate rings.

As Jesus sat opposite these receptacles, he took note of how people were making their contributions. Some hurriedly walked by and threw something in as a matter of habit without giving much thought to the purpose for which they were giving. Others stopped to pick out all of their small change and gave that. Others stopped to read each trumpet carefully and then decided where to give. Some who were taking the most time to carefully scrutinize the receptacles were giving some of the smallest amounts. They were those who looked for their favorite collection basket because they always contributed to the same things over and over again and not to others. There were those who would contribute generously and pause long enough to hear the trumpets clang loudly—and then look around to see if others were looking at them with admiration and envy. It was obvious that these people gave because they enjoyed hearing the trumpets clang and the attention and deference they received.

In the midst of all of this activity, Jesus noticed a certain woman timidly approaching the collection receptacle. She was not particularly good looking or well dressed. There was nothing particularly striking about her. She was just an ordinary woman who could easily become lost in a crowd or walk into a room and not even be noticed. As a matter of fact, the other worshipers—the priests, the Pharisees, and the scribes—walked past her without even noticing her. It took somebody like Jesus to recognize that she was there. She could have easily gone out of the temple that day, as she had done so many times before, without being noticed. Jesus, however, was there that day, and he took notice of her. I doubt if the high priest or members of the Sanhedrin knew her name. But Jesus noticed that she was there.

Sometimes we come to church and we wonder if anybody takes notice of us. We stop in the back or go quietly to our favorite spot. Our names never get called from the pulpit, and we are hardly ever asked to do anything that receives attention. Sometimes people seem to look through us as if we didn't exist. We wonder if anybody knows that we are around. The word that comes to us from the Scripture, however, is that Jesus knows we are here. If nobody else knows—if the pastor doesn't know, if the person sitting next to us doesn't even notice us—Jesus knows we are here. He sees us when we sit down and hears us when we sing praises to his name. If no one else sees or notices, Jesus sees the tears that run silently down our cheeks. He knows we are present.

Not only did Jesus see her; he knew her. He knew what she had been through. He knew what she had and didn't have. He knew that she was a poor widow. As she approached one of the trumpets with her hands shaking and trembling, Jesus noticed that she seemed to be holding something in them. They were two small coins, and when she threw them into one of the trumpets, Jesus recognized them as being two mites. The mite literally means "the thin one" and was the thinnest coin with the smallest value in circulation. It was worth about one-sixteenth of a penny. When she put in her offering, the trumpets did not ring. In fact, you had to be right next to them to even hear the two coins going down. No, those who passed by didn't hear anything when the widow put in her offering. But to the ears of Jesus, the trumpets clanged louder than they had all day. They rang with the clang of faith, the sound of sacrifice, the melody of commitment. They rang with sound of devotion and caring.

Jesus did not disparage or criticize anyone's gift that day. He recognized that many had given generously. Some had even given their best. But the gift of this widow was different from the rest. She and she alone had cared enough to give her all. All of the others had something left after they had given. She had nothing because she had given her all. On the other hand, she had more than the others, for she had the joy and peace that only those who give their all can have and know. She had more than the rest because she had the appreciation of a Savior who recognized that she had given her all. She had her devotion to a God who would take care of her every need because she dared to love God enough and trust God and his Word enough to give her all.

Before she could give her all in terms of money, her heart and her life first had to be given to God. Some define giving in very narrow terms or in terms of money only. They act as if they can buy their way to heaven. They believe that their stewardship should begin and end with their offering, and that after they have given their offering or their tithe, they have given all. They know nothing about rendering service or using their talents because giving for them is a matter of dollars and cents. Others believe that giving consists only of rendering their time and talents in the service of the Lord. They will allow the offering plate to pass them by because they feel they are giving another way—through their time, their talent, and their service. However, to give time and talent without money is not complete stewardship either, especially when God blesses them with all three.

Jesus was right: where our treasures are, so will our hearts be also (Matthew 6:21). As long as we hold our treasures to ourselves, our stewardship is not complete because we are still holding back a part of what we have from God. As long as we hold our treasures to ourselves, we have not given all to God. It is just as one-sided to give service without money as it is to give money without service.

Thus when we talk about tithing, we are not talking simply about giving a tenth of our money but also a tenth of our time and a tenth of our talent as well. It's all right to put an envelope in the plate on Sunday morning, but a gift without the giver is bare. How much of our heart and how much of our lives have we given to God? How much of our time and how much of our treasure is God getting? Are any church organizations getting any of our time and talents? That's how we tithe time and talent. If we work with young people on the job, what about doing some work with the young people in our church? That's how we tithe time and talent. When we bring the skills of our job and the training with which God has blessed us to our church, we tithe time and talent. If we have skills in working with the needy, what about working with them through the missionary society? That's how we tithe time and talent.

If we are retired or at home with nothing to do but feel sorry for ourselves or get on the phone and gossip, how about devoting a few hours each week to the church office? That's tithing time and talent. It might help some of us to get out of the house rather than staying shut indoors and building mental mountains out of physical mole-hills.

Some of us are devoted to community work and helping people outside of the church, and I believe that this is also tithing our time and talent. However, whatever else we do in the community, some of our time and talent still ought to be devoted to the church, for that is bringing the tithe into the storehouse. Thus when we talk about tithing, we are talking about the total stewardship of life—time, talent, and treasure. For unless God gets our time, our talent, and our treasure, then we have not given all.

The widow gave all, and in doing so she blessed Jesus' spirit. As he sat there after a long, draining day of dialogue and debate with the Pharisees and scribes, he saw the shallow gifts of some and the partial gifts of others. His spirit was revived when he saw somebody giving all, for he knew that soon he would have to give his all as well. So far he had been giving his best. He had given his best friendship to the disciples and his best patience to his enemies. He had given his best healing to the sick and his best teaching to the masses. He knew, however, that to truly redeem a sinful world he would have to do more than give his best; he would have to give his all. He would have to be betrayed and denied by his own, deserted by his friends, and lied about by his enemies. He would have to be crowned with a crown of thorns and receive undeserved stripes on his back. He would have to take an old rugged cross on his shoulders and bear it to a lonely hill called Calvary and there, between a weeping glory and a wicked world, he would have to give his all, his very life.

As he stood at the treasury that day watching the partial gifts of people, maybe he asked himself why he should give his all when so many of those for whom he was sacrificing were giving less. But along came a poor widow who cast into the treasury all that she had, and it lifted his spirit to know that there were some who were willing to give their all, just as he was prepared to do. Sometimes when we get discouraged, it helps all of us to know that there is somebody who loves and knows God like we do. And who is to say that on that night when all the disciples deserted him, when he knew that he could have called ten thousand angels to destroy the world and set him free, maybe one of the memories that encouraged his heart and comforted him in his suffering was the thought of this woman who also gave all she had.

It was in giving her all that she blessed the Lord. It was by Jesus giving his all that we have been blessed. The apostle Paul said that Jesus became poor that he might make many rich. He gave up the celestial heights of glory. He gave up the majesty of the royal diadem. He gave up the music of the angelic choir. He gave up the adoration of the heavenly host and became a poor babe born in a manger and wrapped in swaddling clothes. He gave it all up so that we could become rich in salvation, rich in eternal life, rich in faith, rich in hope, rich in love, rich in joy, rich in peace, rich in kindness, rich in patience, rich in gentleness, rich in power, rich in good works. It is only when we give all that we truly bless others and know the joy that comes from giving all. As the hymn says:

You have longed for sweet peace,
And for faith to increase,
And have earnestly, fervently prayed;
But you cannot have rest or be perfectly blest

Until all on the altar is laid.
Would you walk with the Lord in the light of His Word,
And have peace and contentment alway?
You must do His sweet will, to be free from all ill—
On the altar your all you must lay.
Is your all on the altar of sacrifice laid?
Your heart does the Spirit control?
You can only be blest and have peace and sweet rest
As you yield Him your body and soul.[1]

1. Elisha A. Hoffman, "Is Your All on the Altar?"

7. The Beginning of Giving

2 Corinthians 8:1-5

Blessed are those who have enough grace and character, compassion and spirit, even in the midst of their own problems, to give and respond to the needs of others. I remember a conversation that another minister and I once had in which we were discussing how difficult some people can be to work with. He said: "You know, Watley, some of the persons who are the biggest problems to me have a lot of problems themselves." While I agreed with him, I also thought about the fact that some persons with as many problems as the troublemaker in church, in the family, in a social group, or on the job do not become problems for others. A number of us have been greatly inspired and helped by persons with many problems who are still able to look beyond their own world of concern, feel the pain of others, and offer comfort.

While much of the giving in the church and in life comes from those who have the means and resources to offer much without too much stress and strain, it is also true that much comes from those about whom we wonder how they can afford to give what they do. They don't seem to have the ability or means to do what they so often do. For those people who give in spite of the leanness of their personal situation, giving is truly an act of grace, for they are among the most joyful givers. Some people give out of a sense of routine or duty, others because they feel pressured, and still others for show, that they might be complimented for their giving. One can look in the faces of those who give out of their leanness and see joy and pride that is absent from so many others. They are happy to be able to do whatever they can.

I believe that the key to our survival as a race of people has been and will continue to be our ability to give to each other despite the leanness of our personal situations. The persons who helped me go to school, who gave me money when I graduated and at other times simply to encourage me, who gave me odd jobs so that I could earn a little money, were not rich. They worked hard for whatever they had and stretched to make ends meet, just like my family and I were doing. But they were willing to share out of their leanness with me and other young people to encourage us to keep on reaching for higher goals. People who become foster parents or who seek to raise others' children or who try to help the offspring of some young person in the family who made a mistake don't necessarily have more money than others. They are simply able to look beyond their own personal situation. Their hearts are touched by the plight of unwanted, unloved, and abused children, and out of their leanness they share what they have so that young people can have a fighting chance at a decent life. We as African Americans have survived because of the sense of extended family that taught us to feel a responsibility for and kinship with each other. Welfare will not take care of us. No white educational, political, financial, or social system will look out for our best interests. We must take care of each other out of our leanness.

It is only when we stop giving to each other and trying to lift each other up and start becoming jealous of each other, start trying to hold each other down, that we become weak. It's only when we lose our capacity to look beyond our own private world and aspirations and see the leanness of others in our community that we become weak. Consider the situation of the so-called BUPPIE (Black Urban Professional) or BUMPIE (Black Upwardly Mobile Professional) or teacher or administrator with a college degree who speaks fluent English, wears stylish clothes, and lives in a better neighborhood but can still expect to go only so far in the corporation or profession because he or she is black. Then consider the janitor or matron or garbage collector whose English is broken, who barely survives from day to day and week to week, who is exploited and victimized at every turn, who can't get promoted or hired in his or her small sphere, and is discriminated against in the delivery of community services because of his or her dark skin. There is no essential difference between the two. The roles may be different, but the game is the same.

In the time of Paul the churches in the region of Macedonia had been captured by a spirit of giving out of their leanness. During the latter years of his ministry, Paul had become increasingly concerned about the plight of the church in Jerusalem. In a very real sense the Jerusalem church was the mother church of all of the other churches. While many of the younger churches had shown tremendous growth as well as many new problems (for there cannot be growth without problems), the mother church at Jerusalem had fallen on hard times. It was a poor congregation, an old church steeped in whatever traditions there were in the faith. The Holy Spirit laid upon Paul's heart the mission of offering financial assistance to the church at Jerusalem.

This may have seemed like a strange project for Paul to undertake. To begin with, Paul had enough work to do and enough headaches in keeping the scattered congregations intact and on the right track. The churches—Philippi, Galatia, Ephesus, Thessalonica, and Corinth—and their respective problems, as well as young ministers such as Titus and Timothy, provided enough work for a cadre of people. Secondly, one could envision Peter, James, John, or one of the other original twelve disciples, or one of the other saints of the faith such as Barnabas, who had more emotional attachment and direct contact with the church at Jerusalem, leading such a fund-raising venture. But why would Paul, who in spite of his deeds and sacrifices was still regarded as a radical newcomer and looked upon with suspicion by some of the old-timers of the Jerusalem church, undertake such a project? Some of Paul's greatest opposition came from Jerusalem. Some of those who were most insistent that Paul had no right to call himself an apostle were found in Jerusalem. Some of the most conservative members of the early church were found in Jerusalem. Some of the most prejudicial persons regarding the inclusion of Gentiles or foreign people within the faith were in Jerusalem. Some of those who were most insistent that Gentiles come into the church through the route of circumcision as well as other customs of Judaism, in addition to a confession of faith in the lordship of Christ, were in Jerusalem. Some of those who made the biggest speeches about old members and new upstarts, about how "we were here before you got here, so don't come in here with your new ideas and try to change or challenge anything we've been doing because we know the way," were in Jerusalem.

Besides, Paul was not well. He had a physical ailment that he suffered from all of his life, "a thorn in the flesh" that had not been removed. As he grew older, it didn't get better but worse. All that he had done was accomplished under the cross of this handicap. The last thing he needed was a new project. However, Paul was one of those persons who could look beyond his own personal situation and see the needs of others. He had learned to minister to others out of his leanness. He wrote to the church at Philippi: "Not that I complain of want; for I have learned, in whatever state I am, to be content. I know how to be abased, and I know how to abound; in any and all circumstances I have learned the secret of facing plenty and hunger, abundance and want. I can do all things in him [Christ] who strengthens me" (Philippians 4:11-13).

Thus, under the guidance and inspiration of the Holy Spirit, Paul understood the project of trying to raise money for the church in Jerusalem. To do so he did not print up any tickets and try to sell them. He didn't buy any chicken or fish and try to fry it. He did not organize any binges or try to sell any raffles. He did not sponsor any camel trips. When there was a need, Paul wrote the churches and asked them to give from what they had, to share from their leanness and their abundance.

In any financial drive, there are always surprises. Some from whom you would expect the most, give the least, and some from whom you would expect the least, give the most. The church at Corinth had not given all that it could have, and the churches in the region of Macedonia had given far beyond Paul's expectations. Paul testified to the generosity of the Macedonians as he wrote to the church at Corinth. He said: "We want you to know, brethren, about the grace of God which had been shown in the churches of Macedonia, for in a severe test of affliction, their abundance of joy and their extreme poverty have overflowed in a wealth of liberality on their part. For they gave according to their means, as I can testify, and beyond their means, of their own free will, begging us earnestly for the favor of taking part in the relief of the saints—and this, not as we expected, but first they gave themselves to the Lord and to us by the will of God" (2 Corinthians 8:1-5).

The Macedonians had their problems like everyone else. Their country had been overrun and devastated by armies, and the people had lost much of their wealth. They were the least able to help anybody; they needed help themselves. Yet they begged for the opportunity to be part of the offering to help the Jerusalem church. Not only did they do their part; they gave more than their share. They were among the leanest of the lean, and yet they had the most to give and were the most willing to give it. How could they do it? They gave from their leanness in the same way that Paul gave to the Jerusalem church, some of whose members had not been supportive of him. They gave in the same way that Jesus gave up his life for a world that mocked him and for friends who deserted him.

The answer, I believe, is found in the phrase that says, "but first they gave themselves to the Lord" (v. 5). The giving of ourselves wholly to the Lord is the starting point of giving. Until we give ourselves first to the Lord, some of us will always have trouble giving money or anything else to anybody beyond ourselves. Some of us resist tithing not because we don't have it but because we have not given ourselves wholly to the Lord. When we surrender ourselves to the Lord, then tithing is no problem because where the heart is, the treasure is. We realize that our tithe, like us, belongs to the Lord. Some of us think too much is being asked. But when we surrender ourselves wholly to the Lord, we understand that everything we have and everything we are belongs to God. Like the offertory we sometimes sing: "We give Thee but Thine own, What'er the gift may be: / All that we have is Thine alone, A trust, O Lord, from Thee."[1] Or "All things come of Thee, O Lord; and of Thine own have we given Thee."[2]

Some of us don't tithe because we don't think we can afford to do so. But when we give ourselves to the Lord, God's grace will work in our lives and enable us to give, just as it did with the churches of Macedonia. Some of us don't tithe because we don't want people or our friends to talk about us. Anybody who is going to talk about you and doesn't respect the fact that you are trying to obey God's Word is not your friend. When you give yourself to the Lord, people are going to talk. They didn't wake you up this morning. They didn't give you life in your limbs. They didn't love you enough or weren't holy enough to die on Calvary for your sins. And when you come to the end of your journey, they are not going to be the ones to whom you must give an account of your stewardship.

To do whatever is asked, in the right way with the right spirit, whether it's to tithe or sing a solo or serve on a board, we must first give ourselves to the Lord. During this time of stewardship emphasis and season of prayer and fasting, when we examine just how much we are giving from what God has blessed us with, maybe we need to ask ourselves if we have really given ourselves to the Lord. And if so, how much have we given and how much are we holding back? It's only when we've first given ourselves to the Lord that our other giving becomes an act of grace and an experience of joy. It's only when we give ourselves first to the Lord that we can give despite all. Every now and then someone might ask, or we might ask ourselves, why we continue to give in spite of our differences with the preacher or our difficulty with the church. Why are we continuing to give when we're talked about and when others fail to do their part? The answer is simple: a long time ago on our knees, a long time ago walking down the aisle of some church, a long time ago in some city street or country field, we gave ourselves to the Lord. Before the preacher was appointed, before we got caught up in church politics, power struggles, and internecine warfare, before we became a leader, we first gave ourselves to the Lord. On some sickbed or in some trouble, we promised the Lord that if he would deliver us, we'd serve him until our traveling days are done. Since we gave ourselves to the Lord, he's never failed us or forsaken us. He's made ways out of no ways, kept hellhounds at a distance, healed our infirmities, comforted and revived our wounded and broken spirits, helped us pay our bills, answered our prayers, and given us victory when we thought defeat was certain.

Have you given yourself to the Lord? Not to a particular preacher but to the Lord. Not to a certain church or denomination. Not to a certain club. Not to the usher board. Not to the choir. Not to being president or chairperson. Not to raising the most money. To the Lord. That's why we keep on giving—because we first gave ourselves to the Lord. And if we haven't done it, we need to do it now. We need to pray the prayer of the hymn writer:

But drops of grief can ne'er repay
The debt of love I owe:
Here, Lord, I give myself away—
'Tis all that I can do![3]

1. William Walsham How, "We Give Thee But Thine Own."
2. "All Things Come of Thee." Based on 1 Chronicles 29:14b.
3. Isaac Watts, "At the Cross."

8. The Grace of Giving

2 Corinthians 8:7-9

One of the most neglected virtues in the life of the Christian is the grace of giving. We can excel in other virtues and still be devoid and underdeveloped in the grace of giving. This was the problem that Paul was addressing when he wrote the words of our text. Paul had made an appeal to the churches with whom he had a special relationship to assist the church in Jerusalem, which was having a tough time financially. A number of churches had been generous in their response. The church at Corinth, however, had not given according to its potential.

As I have said before, all financial appeals or drives hold surprises. Some persons from whom one might expect little give much, while others from whom one expects much, especially considering their stature as leaders or their lifestyles or the words they speak, give little. This was the case with Paul's financial drive to help the Jerusalem church. The church in the region of Macedonia had given much, though they had little. The Corinthian church, on the other hand, had given little, though they had the potential to give much. Thus Paul wrote to them and told them that he hoped they would develop the grace of giving as they had other virtues. He said, "As ye abound in every thing, in faith, and utterance, and knowledge, and in all diligence, and in your love to us, see that ye abound in this grace also" (2 Corinthians 8:7, KJV). Paul was essentially saying to the Corinthians, "I am pleased and proud of the spiritual strides that many of you have made personally, as well as the growth you have made as a congregation. I am proud of your faith. No individual Christian or congregation can grow or make any great strides without faith in the word, power, and grace of God, as well as what they can accomplish with God."

Paul was proud of their utterance; churches as well as individuals grow through powerful preaching and witnessing. Whenever we see a church that is growing, we can rest assured that some preacher is doing some powerful preaching and some laypersons are doing some mighty witnessing. For it takes both working together to add souls to the Kingdom. A hot pulpit and a cold pew will only be but so effective.

Paul was proud of their knowledge. No individual Christian or congregation can grow without knowledge of the faith. Plants grow not only because of the sun's heat but also because of the sun's light. We need not only the heat of Holy Ghost fire; we need the light of Holy Ghost fire. We need doctrinal teaching as well as evangelistic preaching, *didache* as well as *kerygma,* Bible study as well as joy of the faith, knowledge as well as zeal.

Paul was proud of the diligence of the Corinthians. One does not grow in grace accidentally, nor does one stumble into the Kingdom. But a church as well as an individual has to be diligent, serious, earnest, and intentional about growth. One grows because one is striving for growth. Attaining depth in the things of the Spirit doesn't just happen. Congregation and individuals grow because they are diligent about those things that make for growth. I want to be part of a church that continues to grow deeper, reach higher, and stretch farther. Some may desire a church that believes it has arrived and is content to rest on its tradition. I personally want to be part of a church that says, "I count not myself to have apprehended: but this one thing I do, forgetting those things which are behind, and reaching forth unto those things which are before, I press toward the mark for the prize of the high calling of God in Christ Jesus" (Philippians 3:13-14, KJV).

Paul was also proud of the fact that the Corinthian congregation loved him as he loved them. Individuals grow best when there is closeness to and respect for the shepherd's office. People who are always fighting the preacher usually don't grow much. I've never known churches to grow that are always fighting the preacher, always giving the shepherd a hard time. Such churches tend to have an abundance of confusion, and it's hard for growth to take place in confusion. Growth is an orderly process. Plants grow best when the weather is calm, not during a storm; storms tend to wreck the crops and destroy the field. Whenever a church shows growth, there has been mutual love and respect between the shepherd and the flock.

Yes, there was much that Paul was proud of when he looked at the Corinthian church. That's why he wanted them to grow in the grace of giving, as they had in so many other ways.

Many of us can look at ourselves and see genuine Christian growth. People say things to us and do things to us and we don't get upset like we once did. We are content to let the Lord take care of the situation. We are more secure within and have peace with ourselves, so that people's meanness—the cutting things they say, the little digs they make—really don't upset us like they once did. Sometimes we surprise ourselves because we can remember a time when, if they had done or said such a thing to us, we would have cursed them or knocked them out in a hurry.

Some of us look at our participation in the life of the church and are amazed by our growth. There was a time when we would have been terrified to speak or pray, sing or witness in public. There was a time when we would have been too self-conscious and embarrassed to respond to the Holy Spirit in public. There was a time when we never thought we would be volunteering or offering leadership as we do now. Now we are able to do a number of tasks and function in a variety of capacities with ease.

As we look at how we have grown in grace in so many ways, however, we need to ask ourselves how much we have grown in the grace of giving. Our patience has increased; our prayer life has deepened; our understanding of the faith and the church has expanded; our capacity to love and forgive has expanded; our church attendance, devotion, and sense of responsibility have gotten better; our faith has grown. But how much have we grown in the grace of giving?

Many of us reach a certain point in our giving and stay there. We are like the man who became a millionaire through successful business dealings. One day several of his friends were discussing him. One said, "Getting rich hasn't changed George at all. He still attends church activities." Another friend said, "I agree with you. Getting rich hasn't changed George at all. He used to put a dollar in the collection plate, and he still does."

Where would we be if our faith had stopped growing? How would we have survived that crisis in our career or that bout with illness when it didn't seem as if we would ever get well? But we trusted in the power of God to raise us up again. Where would we be if our faith had stopped growing? We would have never attempted, let alone succeeded, in that venture that others told us could not be done, but by the help of the Lord we did it.

Where would we be if our patience had stopped growing? One thing for sure—a number of us would have walked away from the church and quit our profession a long time ago if our patience had stopped growing.

Where would we be if our knowledge had stopped growing? Where would we be if we had said, "Addition is all I need. I don't need to learn subtraction, multiplication, or division." Where would we be if we had said, "All I need to know is the Psalms. I don't need to know about the Law and the Prophets, the Gospels, the Pauline letters, or the Book of Revelation"?

Where would we be if our love had stopped growing? We would be greedy persons loving only ourselves or selfish persons loving only our families or bigots loving only our race.

Where would we be if our forgiveness had stopped growing? We would be embittered persons still feuding with others over past hurts. We would be small persons who spend our time trying to get even with others who have wronged us. We would diminish our capacity to receive God's forgiveness because we would still pray, "Forgive us our trespasses, as we—if we, when we—forgive those who trespass against us."

Where would we be if we had stopped growing in prayer? Where would we be if we had said, "Now that I know how to say, 'Now I lay me down to sleep, I pray the Lord my soul to keep,' I don't need to learn any other prayer." We would have never learned to say:

Father, I stretch my hands to Thee;
No other help I know;
If Thou withdraw Thyself from me,
Ah! whither shall I go?[1]

If we had stopped growing in prayer, we would have never learned how to fall on our knees and pray until the power of the Lord came down. We would have not known how to pray our way through a crisis until victory came.

If we have not stopped growing in so many other ways, we need to also continue our growth in the grace of giving. We need to hear again the words of Paul, "As ye abound in every thing, in faith, and utterance, and knowledge, and in all diligence, and in your love to us, see that ye abound in this grace also" (2 Corinthians 8:7, KJV).

When I was a boy, I was told that I shouldn't smoke because it would stunt my growth. When it comes to the grace of giving, many of us have stunted growth. We don't tithe or give more not because we're bad, mean, disagreeable, uncooperative, or stubborn people. Our growth has simply been stunted. We've not learned how to truly let go and let God—our growth has been stunted. We have not learned how to trust God's Word without reservation—our growth has been stunted. The negative attitudes and narrow views of others are still determining our actions—our growth has been stunted. Somehow we've been misled into believing that our security depends on our money, and we have not learned the truth that security is relying on God—our growth has been stunted. The devil has told us that if we tithe we will run short, and we have believed him.

Our growth has been stunted because God's Word clearly says that if we tithe, we will be blessed. We've been told that our money and all that we have belong to us, and we have believed it. Our growth has been stunted because God's Word clearly says that "all the tithe . . . is the LORD's: it is holy unto the LORD" (Leviticus 27:30, KJV). We've been told that if we tithe or give we will lose, and we have believed it. Our growth has been stunted because Jesus said, "Give and it will be given to you; good measure, pressed down, shaken together, running over, will be put into your lap" (Luke 6:38).

We are basically good people. We're faithful followers, responsible leaders, people of fervent prayer, inspiring singers, hard workers, and great talkers—but when it comes to the grace of giving, our growth has been stunted. We need to hear again the words of Paul, "As ye abound in every thing, in faith, and utterance, and knowledge, and in all diligence, and in your love to us, see that ye abound in this grace also."

Has our growth been stunted in the grace of giving? Or are we growing in our giving as we ought to be in so many other ways? Have we grown enough to tithe to the Lord? Have we grown enough to give at least 10 percent of all that we have and all that we are to the Lord? Have we grown enough to say, "All that I have and all that I am I give to God and for his service"?

A retired minister whose son was a pilot in the air force received a telegram that read, "Your son David reported missing, believed dead." The heartbroken father fell on his knees and, after agonizing with God, turned the telegram over and wrote on the back the words, "All that I have and all that I am I give to God and for his service." After he prayed, the telephone rang. It was a call from a neighboring university offering the retired pastor a position. On his way to the university, the minister passed an abandoned church with a sign beside it that read For Sale by Auction. He entered the church and, after more prayer, decided to buy it and restore it. He wrote the trustees and made them an offer. A developer had also looked at the property and wanted to buy it and turn it into an amusement arcade. On the day of the auction, as the preacher stood in front of the church, he put his hand in his pocket and found his letter addressed to the trustees. In his confused state of mind that day, he had inadvertently sent the trustees the telegram concerning his son instead of his letter of offer for the church building. He was disappointed and disgusted with himself but decided to stay for the auction anyway. To his surprise, the man in charge of the auction announced that the church had been sold to the minister, who had made the highest offer. He then read from the back of the telegram what he thought was the minister's bid: "All that I have and all that I am I give to God and for his service."[2]

Have we grown in the grace of giving to the point that we can say, "All that I have and all that I am I give to God and for his service"? My body may not be in the best of health and I may not be as strong as other people, but "all that I have and all that I am I give to God and for his service." I'm not perfect. I still make mistakes. I still backslide. I still have weaknesses. The Adversary still trips me up sometimes, but God knows my heart—"All that I have and all that I am I give to God and for his service."

I'm not as young as I used to be. I can't serve or go like I once did. I can't sing like I used to; now my voice cracks. I can't stand at the door and usher like I once did. I can't stand in the kitchen and serve like I once did. But no matter, "All that I have and all that I am I give to God and for his service."

I may not be as talented as someone else. I may not be as educated as someone else. My check or offering may not be as much as someone else's. I may not be as experienced or seasoned as the next person, but that's all right because "all that I have and all that I am I give to God and for his service."

That's still the highest offer, for that's the offer that Jesus made on Calvary when he redeemed us from our sins with his own precious blood. Paul says, "For ye know the grace of our Lord Jesus Christ, that, though he was rich, yet for your sakes he became poor, that ye through his poverty might be rich" (2 Corinthians 8:9, KJV). "All that I have and all that I am I give to God and for his service." That's the grace of Jesus, and that's the grace of giving.

> All to Jesus I surrender, all to Him I freely give;
> I will ever love and trust Him, in His presence daily live.
> I surrender all, I surrender all,
> All to Thee, my blessed Savior, I surrender all.[3]

1. Charles Wesley, "Father, I Stretch My Hands to Thee."
2. Adapted from G. Curtis Jones, *1000 Illustrations for Preaching and Teaching* (Nashville: Broadman Press, 1986), 330.
3. J. W. Van DeVenter, "I Surrender All."

9. Give Till It Feels Good

2 Corinthians 9:7

Most of us have heard the expression "Give till it hurts." This plea is based on the fact that most of us give from our excess; we give by skimming off the top. Most of us give at a level at which we really don't miss very much of what we give. We give what is known as our spare change. One Sunday morning when I was pastoring my first church in Georgia, I announced that it was time to receive the missionary offering. I heard someone seated behind me say, "Good, now's my chance to get rid of these pennies." A number of us are still giving to the Lord that which essentially costs us little or nothing.

This attitude toward giving is seen not only in terms of the monetary offerings we bring to the church but other kinds of gifts as well. If a community is hit by a storm or tornado, when a family is burned out, or when a general appeal is made to help the needy, observe the kinds of contributions that some people make. Some people look on appeals for clothes as an opportunity to get rid of all the junk in their closets, attics, or basements. Some persons give clothes that are so dirty and greasy they will never become clean or so ragged that no one could possibly wear them. Giving clothes that are good but a little out of style is one thing; giving away something that is good because our taste has changed is one thing; giving away something that is good that we've outgrown is one thing—especially when we know that we'll never be that size again in this life! However, giving away clothes that are ragged and worn out is another matter.

Some of us give away food the same way. If we don't want to eat food with an expired date, what makes us think the less fortunate

58

want it? When many of us donate food, we reach to the back or bottom of the cabinet or pantry and get out some dusty or dented can containing something we don't want or like and give that away.

Some of us give our service the same way. We will accept only those responsibilities that we can discharge in our spare time. We don't want to do anything that's going to require that we expend some serious time and attention. A number of persons will not do anything that requires serious commitment.

There is another level of giving, however, known as sacrificial giving. People know when they have given at this level because their gift makes a dent in their pocketbooks, time, or resources. At this level we give not from our reserves but from our operating capital. Thus people are encouraged to dig down deep and "give till it hurts." I have problems with this expression, however, because some of us don't have to give very much before we start hurting! Some of us start hurting after we give twenty-five or fifty cents, no matter how much abundance we may have. Some of us start hurting after we give one dollar. Others of us hurt after we give five or ten dollars. Some of us don't have to give anything to hurt; we start hurting when the very subject of giving is brought up. It hurts so much for some of us to give that even if we have something that we have not used in years, and the probability is great that we will never use it again, we would still prefer to hold onto it and let it sit in a trunk and collect dust rather than give it to someone who can use it. It hurts some of us so much to give that we would rather let good clothes dry-rot, mildew, and become moth-eaten than give them away. It hurts some of us so much to give that we would rather let food go bad as it sits in our freezers and on our shelves than give it away to those less fortunate.

Our goal should not be to give till it hurts but to give till it feels good. As the words of our text remind us, "Each of you must give as you have made up your mind, not reluctantly or under compulsion, for God loves a cheerful giver" (2 Corinthians 9:7, NRSV). In order to be able to give till it feels good, let us be clear about what Paul said and what he didn't say. Paul wrote, "Each of you must give as you have made up your mind." Paul did not write, "Each of you must give as your neighbor gives." Nothing can rob us of the joy of giving as quickly as comparing our giving with our neighbor's. We can give the best we can and feel good about it, but then we start comparing our gift with others. If others give much more than we, if we are not careful, we will begin to feel ashamed and despise our gift. Once the devil begins to make us feel ashamed of our gift, then the devil has won the victory by taking the joy out of giving. Once we lose the joy of giving, we may not even do what we can. We will say, "Why should I give? My little won't be missed."

However, we must never allow anyone to cheapen our gifts, including ourselves. When we read the Scriptures, we observe that Jesus never cheapened anyone's gift, no matter how little or how much it was. When he wanted to feed five thousand, a little boy brought him a lunch of two fish and five barley loaves. There were those who asked, "What is that among so many?" Jesus, however, accepted the gift, gave thanks for it, and fed the multitudes. When a woman anointed Jesus with an alabaster flask of expensive oint- ment, there were those who cheapened the gift and called it a waste. Jesus, however, accepted the gift and declared that whenever the gospel was preached, her gift would be talked about. There were those who would have cheapened the widow's two mites, but Jesus declared that because she had given her all, she had given more than all the rest. "Each of you must give as you have made up your mind, not reluctantly or under compulsion, for God loves a cheerful giver."

We can lose the joy of giving by comparing our gifts with others'. We can make a sacrificial gift and feel good—and then look at the little that others who could give more are giving and get mad. We find ourselves asking the question, "Why should I strain myself to give when some of the so-called big shots and leaders are doing so little?" Well, we can't give out of someone else's pocketbook. They may be able to do better, but until they allow the Lord to speak to their hearts and the Spirit to move them, there's nothing we can do about it. So it makes no sense to frustrate ourselves by allowing someone else's cheapness to take the joy out of our generosity. We know how good God has been to us. We know how God has blessed us. We know how God has kept his word to us. Therefore we give because we have received from God, irrespective of what others do. To keep the joy of giving we must not allow Satan to force us into playing the comparison game. "Each of you must give as you have made up your mind, not reluctantly or under compulsion, for God loves a cheerful giver."

It feels good when we give what we have. That's why tithing feels so good—because it is not based on any specific predetermined amount. It is based on what we have. If my income is one hundred dollars and I give ten, or if my allowance is fifty cents and I give a nickel, then I have given as much proportionately as the person whose income is one thousand dollars and puts in one hundred. I need not feel inferior because of my ten dollars or nickel, and the person who gives one hundred dollars has no right to feel superior, for that person has given no more based on his or her income than I have based on mine. As a matter of fact, the person who gives much is simply following Scripture: "From everyone to whom much has been given, much will much be required" (Luke 12:48, NRSV). Therefore, before we complain about having to give much, maybe we ought to think about the fact that we've received much— for we couldn't give it if we hadn't received it.

Paul wrote, "Each of you must give as you have made up your mind, not reluctantly or under compulsion." He did not say, "Each of you must give based on your bills and expenses." Trying to make a decision to tithe or give more based on our bills or obligations is like trying to walk on water by looking at the wind and the waves. Peter discovered some two thousand years ago that he could not walk steadily through a storm, he could not walk on water, by looking at the wind and the waves. The only way he could walk on water through a storm was by looking at Jesus. Looking at Jesus didn't make the storm disappear. Looking at Jesus didn't make the winds subside and the rolling billows cease. Looking at Jesus helped Peter keep firm and sure footing in the midst of the storm. Looking at Jesus meant that Peter would not sink.

If we looked at our obligations, a number of us would not give at all, let alone tithe. A number of us are already on the verge of sinking. Trying to make ends meet is a very delicate balancing act for most of us. It's like trying to find firm footing in the midst of a stormy sea. To tithe does not mean that one has forgotten about the storm. Tithers have not forgotten about their bills. To tithe doesn't mean that our bills will automatically disappear. Those who tithe simply understand that there is another Power at work in the midst of life's storms. Winds and waves obey his will. In other words, he is able to make a way out of no way through life's financial storms.

We don't know what tomorrow will bring in terms of stormy weather. We don't know how turbulent the seas will yet become. But this we know—if we keep our eyes on Jesus, we cannot sink. If we keep our eyes on Jesus, no rolling wave can take us under, and no strong wind can blow us over.

Paul wrote, "Each of you must give as you have made up your mind, not reluctantly or under compulsion." He did not write, "Each of you must give according to your pocketbook." As we cannot give solely on the basis of the bills we see, neither can our giving be based solely on the resources we see. As God's children we must never forget that we have resources unseen. As a matter of fact, our unseen resources are greater than the resources we can see. Paul wrote: "For our light affliction, which is but for a moment, worketh for us a far more exceeding and eternal weight of glory; while we look not at the things which are seen, but at the things which are not seen: for the things which are seen are temporal; but the things which are not seen are eternal" (2 Corinthians 4:17-18, KJV). Bills that we see are light afflictions that soon pass away. We make one and work to pay it off so that we can make others, and the process continues. The money that we see is temporal and will soon pass away. It doesn't stay with us forever. We make it to spend it. Money comes and goes, but God's unseen power stays with us. We have unseen resources—"The eternal God is thy refuge, and underneath are the everlasting arms" (Deuteronomy 33:27, KJV). Money comes and goes, but the unseen presence of Christ never leaves us. We have resources unseen, for Jesus has promised never to leave us alone. Money comes and goes, but the unseen keeping power of the Holy Ghost is eternal. We have resources unseen.

That's the only way some of us have made it: we've had resources unseen. How do you explain the survival of an African people who were brought to these shores as chattel and worked for over four hundred years and then freed without so much as even forty acres and a mule to compensate them? We've had resources unseen. That's how some of us have survived as couples, raised our children, and made it in a system that was dead set against us. We've had resources unseen. How do you explain the victory of Martin Luther King Jr. and a few Bible-carrying, hymn-singing, black church people over the powerful forces of segregation in the Jim Crow South? They had resources unseen. What keeps the flame of freedom alive in the hearts of oppressed people throughout the world? What keeps their hopes alive? Where do they receive the strength to keep on struggling under cruel and tyrannical regimes? They have resources unseen. As we sacrifice and give, struggle and labor on behalf of the kingdom of God, let us never forget that we have resources unseen.

"Each of you must give as you have made up your mind, not reluctantly or under compulsion, for God loves a cheerful giver." Giving out of a sense of comparison or competition doesn't feel good because that kind of giving comes from the ego. Giving by looking at our bills or resources doesn't feel good because that kind of giving comes from the head. Giving grudgingly doesn't feel good because it's done sparingly. Necessity giving doesn't feel good because it's done from fear. Giving feels good only when it comes from the heart. True giving is not simply a matter of the pocketbook; it's a matter of the heart. Giving from the heart is cheerful giving. Giving from the heart is the giving of love. And it feels good to love. That's why God loves the cheerful giver—because such is the giving of love. God not only loves the cheerful giver, but the cheerful giver loves God.

It is said that poet Robert Louis Stevenson was loved by his servants. One would awaken him every morning with a cup of tea. On one occasion his usual attendant was off duty, and another took his place. The servant woke him not only with a cup of tea but also with a carefully cooked omelette. Stevenson thanked him and said, "Great is your forethought." "No," said the servant, "great is my love."

That's why some of us enjoy giving: because when we think about how good God has been to us, great is our love. That's why we sacrifice and give even when we can't afford to—great is our love. That's why we continue to serve even when our work goes unrecognized and unheralded—great is our love. That's why we go on giving even when we're talked about and criticized—great is our love. When we think about how far the Lord has brought us—great is our love. When we think about the sacrifice of Jesus on Calvary—great is our love.

10. Honey from a Lion

Judges 14:5-9

When asked, "What part of the worship service do you like the least?" or "If you had your choice, what part of the service would you cut out?" a number of people would answer, "The offering." As tiresome and unexciting as the announcements may be, as off-key as some of the singing may be, as long and awful as some of the preaching may be, all of these are still preferable to the offering. For a number of persons, the offering is the most painful part of the worship service. The only relief or pleasure that some people derive from the offering is knowing that they are one step closer to the end of the service.

The offering is painful for some people because they don't want to give to the church at all. They believe that church ought to be free. They have no problem paying seven dollars to get into the movies, or twenty-five or thirty dollars to hear some performer or attend some sporting event. They have no problem paying for the meal they receive in the restaurant, the bill they owe at the hotel, the food they buy in the grocery store, the gas they get at the service station, or the clothes they wear. But they become angry, offended, and resistant to giving an offering in church.

Some people are pained by the offering because they feel guilty about what they give. They know they are not giving God a fair and proportionate share of their income. They know they are not giving according to God's Word. Thus they feel a little sheepish and uncomfortable when the offering plate is passed to them. Some people are pained by the offering because they are ashamed of what they give. Some people feel badly because they are not able to give what others give or what is being asked.

Out of all of those who are pained by the offering, my heart goes out to those who are ashamed of their gifts. Often these are the ones who truly love the Lord, the church, and their pastor, because if they didn't, they wouldn't feel badly about what they give. To this group I cannot emphasize enough: never feel ashamed because you can't give more than what you have. No one ought to feel ashamed of his or her gift when it's that person's best. God is not ashamed of your best; so don't you be ashamed of your best either.

Although the offering is received in the midst of worship, for many people it is really not an act of worship. When it is received before the sermon, it is viewed as part of the preliminaries that one must sit through before the real worship starts. I must confess that I have been guilty of thinking at times, as many of you have, "Let's hurry up and get the offering out of the way so that we can get down to the real business of worship." When the offering is received after the sermon, we look on it as another procedure, distinct from real worship, that we must go through before we can go home. How many times have we all heard it said, "Now we're going to interrupt the order of our service and take an offering?"

For some people the offering is like a time-out in the service. It's the time to pass notes, speak to people, go outside for a smoke, or get up and walk around and model what we have on. If we don't shout, if we're not moved or led to come to the altar or mourner's bench, if we are not playing any part in the worship service and have no messages to personally bring to the pulpit, then the offering is the best time to walk around and be seen. For some people the offering is the time to leave. A number of congregations thin out considerably during the offering. One of the most difficult aspects of leading worship in some churches is that of trying to maintain a sense of order and sacredness during the offering. I've seen many services that were orderly and flowing smoothly break down into disarray at offering time. I've seen services that were Spirit-filled and powerful lose all of their sacredness at offering time.

Discovering the joy of giving or learning to view the offering as a sacred act of divine worship is like trying to get honey from a lion, or pleasure from that which usually causes us pain, or sweetness from that which we tend to regard with hostility, fear, and suspicion. In our text Samson managed to do just that. Samson was engaged in one of his favorite activities—he was on his way to see a woman.

He may have been strong enough to pick up the huge main gates to the city of Gaza and carry them off. He may have been powerful enough to slay a thousand Philistines with the jawbone of an ass. However, he had no willpower or strength when confronted by a pretty face, a soft voice, and a nice figure. Samson, though physically strong, had a spiritual weakness that would one day cause his downfall.

Despite the many good and noble qualities we may have, all of us have points of weakness, a moral Achilles' heel that, if we don't get it under control, will lead to our undoing. I'm not referring just to sins of the flesh. Haughtiness of spirit and attitude, hardness of heart, proclivities toward vicious gossip, unforgiveness toward those who have wronged us, jealousy toward those we feel threatened by, gluttony, and greed—all will warp our personalities, sap our joy, shorten our lives, and send us to hell, just like the sins of the flesh.

Samson was going to see a woman, unaware of the dangers ahead. As he went on his merry way, a lion came out of the woods and attacked him. The Word tells us that the Spirit of God came mightily upon Samson, who slew the lion with his bare hands. When Samson needed God's Spirit and power, they were there to save him. Although Samson was far from living the life of holiness that his Nazarite vow called for, when Samson needed God's presence, God was there. In spite of his weakness, Samson was still God's man with a special role to play in the history of Israel. Therefore God would not let him be destroyed. God's power is always present to save his children. No one is destroyed by sin or defeated by the Adversary without his or her consent and cooperation. God's power is always present to protect and defend God's own.

If God defended Samson, God will also take care of us. I know that we sometimes wonder how we're going to make it if we tithe. All around us are financially consuming lions ready to eat up our income. With children in school, with mortgages and car notes, with sickness and tenuous employment situations, how can we possibly tithe? When we're on a fixed income and prices keep going up, how can we possibly tithe? When we're facing retirement and know that our income will be cut in half, how can we possibly tithe? We have no great resources to fall back on. When we look at what we face and what little we have to fight with, how can we possibly tithe—or donate to Women's Day, Men's Day, the church anniversary, or any other special appeal? When we look at our few resources, we can no more do it than a man can slay a lion with his bare hands.

In and of ourselves we cannot, and God knows that we cannot. That's why God gives his Holy Spirit and power. God will help us handle our lions. If God helped Samson when he was on a pleasure trip, if we're trying to do right and live and give according to God's Word, God will not be so callous as to leave us. We don't have to fear the lions of this life. Whether they be male or female, black or white, employer or coworker, human or demonic, financial or political, personal or social, physical or spiritual, God will help us be victorious over our lions.

Let us never forget that God knows how to handle lions. Sometimes God will strengthen our hands to do whatever has to be done to master our problem. God will provide ways for us to slay our lions. Sometimes, as was the case with David, God will give us a rod and a staff to fight our lions. Sometimes God will send us a friend as a rod and extra blessings as a staff to help us fight our lions. There are those of us who know what it is like to have bills to pay and not know how we are going to pay them, only to go to the mailbox and receive an unexpected blessing. Those are God's rods and staffs given to us to help us fight our lions.

Sometimes, like Daniel, we won't have to fight at all. God's power will lock the jaws of lions, and they won't be able to touch us. The Adversary will cause all kinds of financial crises to arise. Our livelihood will be cut off, our business will take a nosedive, our paycheck will be cut, people will do mean things to us, but in the midst of all that happens, God will preserve us and lions won't be able to touch us. We wonder how some people are making it and surviving with all their bills. The answer is simple: God is keeping them, and the lions can't touch them. Never fear lions. Our God knows how to handle lions in all situations.

God's Spirit came mightily upon Samson. God's Spirit strengthened Samson's arms and fortified his courage. Samson defeated the lion because he was led and empowered by God's Spirit. No life is as powerful as the Spirit-led and Spirit-filled life. No singing is as inspiring as Spirit-filled singing. No preaching is as moving as Spirit-led preaching. No testimony is as convincing as the Spirit-filled testimony. No giving is like Spirit-led giving. How was Jesus able to give so much and do so much in such a short period of time? He was filled and led by the Spirit. In the church we have many kinds of giving: pressured giving, dutiful giving, giving for show, giving out of guilt, sincere giving, self-giving, thanksgiving. I would propose another kind of giving, and that is Spirit-led giving.

What is Spirit-led giving? Spirit-led giving occurs when we earnestly seek God's direction as to what we should give and then ask God's help in making a way for us to give it. So many times we look at our budgets and decide what we can or cannot do, forgetting that God who owns the cattle on a thousand hills has promised to supply all of our needs according to his riches in glory. We must never underestimate the importance of being led by the Spirit, "for all who are led by the Spirit of God are children of God" (Romans 8:14, NRSV). Many of us are like Peter, who started walking toward Jesus on the water in the midst of a storm. As long as he kept his eyes on Jesus, he could walk on the water, but when he took his eyes off Jesus and started looking at the wind and the waves, he began to sink. Some of us don't give more because we keep looking at the wind; we keep our eyes on our bills. But if we look to Jesus and are led by his Spirit, I'm a witness to the fact that the winds of life can't blow you away.

After slaying the lion, Samson made it to his destination. On his return trip, he decided to turn aside to see the lion he had slain. (We also must be careful about what we do and say while trying to reach our destination because there's always a return trip when we must pass by some of the same places and people and face the results of our previous journey.) As Samson neared the carcass, he discovered life and activity in the body of the lion: a swarm of bees had settled there and built a honeycomb. Samson gathered the honey and ate some of it as he continued his journey; he also gave some to his parents when he reached home. Samson found honey not just in any lion but in the same lion that attacked him. Samson found honey in the same lion that had been an obstacle and an impediment in his path. Samson found honey in the same lion that he had slain with God's help.

Don't let giving be a stumbling block on your Christian journey. Some people would rather do anything than part with some of their earthly treasure. They'll sing, they'll serve, they'll attend meetings, they'll even try to live a halfway decent life. But they will not dig deep into their pockets and give. And yet giving is the basis of our faith. God gives; Jesus gives; the Holy Spirit gives; we too must give. When our giving is led by the Spirit, what is an impediment to some becomes a pleasure to us, that which nourishes and replenishes rather than defeats us. When we give, we gather handfuls of honey. "Give, and it will be given to you; good measure, pressed down, shaken together, running over" (Luke 6:38). When we are led by the Spirit, what is painful to others becomes joy to us from which we gather handfuls of honey. The writer of the book of Hebrews reminds us of what Jesus gave and the honey he received from his Spirit-led giving: "Looking unto Jesus the author and finisher of our faith; who for the joy that was set before him endured the cross, despising the shame, and is set down at the right hand of the throne of God" (Hebrews 12:2, KJV).

Instead of finding only the body of a dead lion, Samson found so much more. He found honey in that lion, which sweetened his journey. What a surprise! Our faith is full of surprises in which we find much more than we expected. What a surprise for the shepherds who went to work one night expecting nothing and instead saw angels and heard glad tidings about a newborn Savior! What a surprise for Zacharias, who went into the temple and met the angel Gabriel, who told him that his barren wife would give birth to a son whose name would be called John and would become a new Elijah for his people! What a surprise for Mary and Martha to discover that Jesus had not come too late but that he is the resurrection and the life and could raise their brother, who had been dead four days! What a surprise for the early church when it was in prayer for Peter's deliverance and he came and knocked on the door because even as they prayed, God's angel had set him free! What a surprise for the disciple John to discover that he was not alone on Patmos because Jesus, the exalted Lord, who was dead but was alive forevermore, was with him! What a surprise the women received who went to the tomb to anoint the dead body of Jesus only to discover that he was not there but had risen just like he said he would! It's like receiving honey from a lion.

What a surprise to discover that when we give, we don't lose. Paul said, "For me to live is Christ, and to die is gain" (Philippians 1:21). That's receiving honey from a lion. That's being blessed in abundance in places and ways that we wouldn't expect.

In the carcass of the lion, whom God's power had helped him slay, Samson found honey. Our God is not only powerful; our God is sweet. The psalmist said: "O taste and see that the LORD is good" (Psalm 34:8). We serve a sweet Savior. In Georgia we used to sing:

Sweet Jesus, Sweet Jesus;
He's the lily of the valley, the bright and morning star,
Sweet Jesus, sweet Jesus;
He's the joy of my salvation, Praise his name.[1]

1. Traditional spiritual.

11. Everything Has Its Price

2 Samuel 24:22-25

There is a story of a man who went to visit his relatives. On the day of his arrival, they cooked up and served a large batch of freshly fried chicken. The next day, they served the leftover chicken, but still they did not eat it all. Consequently, on the third day, they still had chicken to serve their visiting relative. As we are all aware, even the best fried chicken in the world loses some of its zest after it has been warmed over a couple of times. On the third day, chicken that has been twice warmed over tastes just like what it is—chicken that has been twice warmed over. Realizing this, his hostess said to him, "I guess you're tired of chicken by now." He looked at her and said, "Don't make me no difference as long as its free."

There is much goodness in life—from the wonders and beauties of nature to the divine rights bestowed on us through the goodness and grace of God, from the natural human rights of all men and women to the constitutional rights granted to us by the law of this land in which we live. We enjoy all this goodness, often with no personal cost to us.

There are some people, however, whose enjoyment of anything is directly related to how little it costs them. If it's free, whatever it is, it's okay. No matter how bad it is, whether they need it or not, want it or not, like it or not—if it's free, they'll take it. I've seen people take food home from church to be put in refrigerators that are already full of leftovers. Many times the food stays there until it turns bad and has to be thrown away. Some of these people knew that they already had more food than they could eat. Some knew that they probably weren't going to eat what they were taking home. Why did they take it? Because it was free. For these people the best things in life really are free!

We would be mistaken, however, to believe that things that cost us nothing are free. Everything in life costs something. And if some things come to us without cost, the reason is simple: Somebody paid a price so that we might freely enjoy them. We may be able to enjoy the moon and stars, the blooming flowers, and the songs of birds without cost, but Somebody paid a price for us to enjoy them. According to Genesis, "In the beginning God created the heavens and the earth. The earth was without form and void, and darkness was upon the face of the deep; and the Spirit of God was moving over the face of the waters. And God said, 'Let there be light'; and there was light" (Genesis 1:1-3). The writer concludes the Creation narrative by saying, "Thus the heavens and the earth were finished, and all the host of them. And on the seventh day God finished his work which he had done, and he rested on the seventh day from all his work which he had done" (Genesis 2:1-2). God labored to give us the universe. People who want something for nothing desire what even God doesn't have. God worked, labored, and sacrificed to give us the world—and our faith—as we know it. The glow of the moon, the light of the stars, the beauty of flowers, and the sweet melodies of the birds are free because God paid the price of labor and expended divine energy and power so that we could enjoy them.

Anyone who knows anything at all about love knows that it is not free. Love is something that we must work at, invest in, sacrifice for, and give to in order to have. Anyone who wants to keep everything for self will not know love. Anybody who is too cheap to give up some independence and ego, some time, some talent and money, and some hopes and desires for the sake and well-being of somebody else will never know the meaning of love. People whose relationships and marriages we admire had to pay a price. They had to make some sacrifice for the sake of their relationship. They had to bend sometimes when they didn't feel like it. They had to forgive each other and love each other despite imperfections of character and physical weaknesses and flaws. People who are well loved and admired had to pay a price. You don't receive love from others by being selfish. You have to be prepared to give to others, show concern for others, invest some precious time and energy and resources on behalf of others, if you would receive the love of others. Love is not free but costly.

Never believe that the rights and privileges we enjoy have come to us without cost. If African Americans have the right to speak our minds, assemble without fear, and worship God in freedom, somebody had to pay a price. If we are able to vote and run for elected offices, somebody had to pay a price. If we can live basically wherever we can afford to live, somebody had to pay a price. If we can work in every major industry and become members of any profession, somebody had to pay a price. If we can attend school and have the vast reservoirs of human knowledge opened to us, then somebody had to pay a price. If we can stay at any hotel we can afford, participate in any sport as either a player or spectator, engage in any other form of entertainment, or eat at any restaurant, somebody had to pay a price.

In every war that this country has fought to secure these rights, black blood has flowed with the blood of others. Somebody did pay a price. In graves marked and unmarked lie the remains of people of color who dared to get out of their prescribed place and receive the hostile reaction of a racist society. Somebody did pay a price. If you are not the first black to work for the company where you're employed or to occupy the position that you hold, then some black person who was the first paid a price for you. And if you are the first African American, female, young or old person, or disabled individual to be where you are, then you are paying the price for somebody else to enjoy freely what is costing you so much in terms of pocketed insults, bigoted attitudes, and sometimes thwarted goals and frustrated ambitions.

The faith that has been passed down from generation to generation did not come to us without cost. Religion has never been a free enterprise; sacrifice is inherent in the very nature of religion. From the very beginning, women and men made sacrifices and gave offerings to God as they prayed for blessings, sought help, and gave thanks. From the very beginning, giving was a part of worship. From the very beginning, it was believed that one ought not come before God empty-headed, empty-hearted, or empty-handed. It was believed that if one was coming to God to give thanks, then one ought to offer an expression of praise and gratitude. For how can one truly be thankful to God without being willing and happy about giving an offering of thanks?

Some people ask, "Why should I give to the church? The church won't miss my two dollars and fifty cents." Some people say, "If God owns the cattle on a thousand hills, why does God need my five dollars?" We give not because the church would close its doors if we didn't give. The church existed long before we received a box of offering envelopes and, unless the Second Coming occurs in our lifetime, it will continue to exist long after we stop using them. We give because God has blessed us individually, and thus we make our individual expressions of thanksgiving and praise. We give not because heaven or the church would go bankrupt if we kept our money in our pockets. Many a person has stopped giving, and to their dismay the church has continued to prosper. What they don't realize is that when they stop, the Holy Spirit moves somebody else's heart to start. Our offering is our act of witness: "I may not be able to speak or sing like somebody else, but one thing I can do: I can give as God has blessed me."

When one is coming to God looking for help, one ought not come empty-handed. If we want to receive all that someone has to offer, then we ought at least be willing to give something in return. Nobody, not even heaven, appreciates a freeloader—someone who wants to receive all and give little or nothing. Whenever we ask for anything, we ought to be willing to give something in return. What we have may be little or much, but we ought to offer it anyhow. We ought to be prepared to give to others as we desire others to give to us.

Certainly if we are coming to God seeking forgiveness, we should not come empty-handed. We ought not come without an expression that represents our labors, that costs us, that says, "I'm sorry for what I've done. I'm not trying to buy your forgiveness. I'm just offering something that costs me to let you know how sorry I am." This was the attitude that motivated David to utter the words of our text. David had sinned against God, and he, along with the people of Israel who had consented and cooperated in David's sin, were reaping God's wrath. Many of us would never start a rumor or lie or gossip, but we would consent to it by our eagerness to hear and cooperate by passing it along. Many of us would never lift a hand to throw a stone, but, like Saul in the book of Acts, we would hold the coats of those doing the stoning. However, there is a penalty for consent and cooperation, as there is for initiation. The judgment upon the Nazi war criminals in the trials at Nuremberg is that there is a penalty for consent and cooperation as well as for initiation.

That's why Jesus told us that we would give an account for every vain or idle word that we speak.

Because David had initiated the sin and the people had consented and cooperated, God's judgment had come upon them in the form of a pestilence that had moved throughout the land and was approaching the city of Jerusalem. As David beheld the avenging angel coming toward the city, he prayed for his people: "Lo, I have sinned, and I have done wickedly; but these sheep, what have they done? Let thy hand, I pray thee, be against me and against my father's house" (2 Samuel 24:17). The sheep have done nothing but follow their shepherd. They may have been wrong in following down a wrong path and offering no protest. But still they only followed, said David, while I led.

The Lord heard David's prayer, forgave him (as God always will when the prayer is from the heart), and sent the prophet Gad to him. Gad told David to build an altar on the threshing floor of Araunah the Jebusite. Araunah was hard at work threshing wheat when he saw David approaching him. Araunah stopped his work and, after giving the proper respect, inquired as to why the king had come. When David told him that he had come to build an altar so that the plague might be averted, Araunah said, "Whatever I have is yours. I give you the threshing floor as sacred ground. I give the oxen as sacrifice. I give you my wooden tools and open yokes as wood. I give you the sledge as fuel. All of this I give free of charge." But David could not accept the offer. Why not? Because, he explained, "I will not offer burnt offerings to the LORD my God which cost me nothing" (see 2 Samuel 24:22-24). In other words, if I accepted your offer, then even though I would be speaking the words, the sacrifice would be yours. The sin was mine; the prayer was mine; the sacrifice ought to be mine. Salvation will not come to me by relying on somebody else's sacrifice. If I am to be truly blessed and forgiven, then I must sacrifice and give that which costs me something.

In order to give us this covenant relationship with God in which we now stand, our ancestor Abraham had to become a wandering nomad and journey by faith in search of a land that God promised would one day belong to his descendants. In order to teach us the lesson of what it means to trust God without reservation, long ago Abraham was prepared to sacrifice his only son, Isaac. But an angel stopped him, even as the angel has withheld his hand from the destruction of Jerusalem. In order to give us the law, Moses had to pay the price of giving up a bright future as a son of Pharaoh's household to assume the thankless task of liberator. In order to give us the land in which we dwell, Joshua had to spend his days fighting to posses it. We cannot exist on their sacrifices. Our salvation and forgiveness has its own price, which we must pay. "I will not offer burnt offerings to the LORD my God which cost me nothing."

Then, when I think about how good God has been to me, how far God has brought me, how long God has kept me, and how much longer God may have to keep me, "I will not offer burnt offerings to the LORD my God which cost me nothing." When God has given me the most, how can I give him the least? When I think about how God brought me from being a shepherd boy to the throne of Israel, "I will not offer burnt offerings to the LORD my God which cost me nothing." When I think about how God kept me safe from marauding lions and ravenous wolves, "I will not offer burnt offerings to the LORD my God which cost me nothing." When I think about when Samuel came to my father's house to anoint another king to replace Saul, and how everybody overlooked me and forgot about me but God remembered and chose me, the least, as the next king, then "I will not offer burnt offerings to the LORD my God which cost me nothing." When I remember how God gave me victory over Goliath, who laughed at me, and protected me from Saul, who hunted me, and kept me from vengeance when Saul was delivered into my hands, then "I will not offer burnt offerings to the LORD my God which cost me nothing." When I remember how God gave me victory over enemies without and within my own household, even when my own son, Absalom, rose up against me and drove me from my throne, but the Lord restored me, "I will not offer burnt offerings to the LORD my God which cost me nothing."

When I think about the fact that the Lord has been and continues to be my shepherd,

> . . . I shall not want;
>   he makes me lie down in green pastures.
> He leads me besides still waters;
>   he restores my soul.
> He leads me in paths of righteousness
>   for his name's sake.

Even though I walk through the valley of the shadow of death,
   I fear no evil;
[God is] with me;
[God's rod and staff] comfort me. . . .
[God anoints] my head with oil,
   my cup overflows.
Surely goodness and mercy shall follow me
   all the days of my life;
and I shall dwell in the house of the LORD
   for ever. (Psalm 23)

When I think about all of that, "I will not offer burnt offerings to the LORD my God which cost me nothing." Before we complain about the high price of religion, before we complain about tithes and offerings, before we complain about how much we are called upon to give, think about how much God has given and, if we're fair, we will say like David, "I will not offer burnt offerings to the LORD my God which cost me nothing."

12. God Keeps Promises

2 Kings 7:1-2

No matter how illogical or impossible its promises or predictions may seem or sound, we must be careful about disbelieving or doubting, mocking or making light of the Word of God.

This is the lesson we learn from the story surrounding our text. Israel and Syria had been in protracted warfare, and a siege had been instituted against the city of Samaria. The siege was the ancient equivalent of our modern embargo. If a city was considered to be too well fortified to be taken in battle, the opposing army would try to surround it and cut off its flow of food, supplies, and commerce. The opposing army then waited for the food, water, and other provisions of the city under siege to run out. When the inhabitants became sufficiently demoralized or weakened through starvation and isolation, the army would attack the city. Sometimes a city under siege fell without a fight.

The siege was common military strategy of that era—and was very effective. No one knew, however, how long a siege would last. No one knew how long the supplies of a city would last or how long its inhabitants could hold out. The opposing army knew, however, that cities under siege could not hold out forever. Thus victory was only a matter of time. If the opposing army had the patience to wait and watch, then victory would be theirs. During a siege there were times when nothing seemed to be happening; little or no progress was evident. However, every day that the opposing army could be vigilant and patient brought it one day closer to victory. The success of a siege consisted of days piled upon days of waiting and working, faithfulness and patience, when nothing seemed to be happening. If an army wanted an immediate victory, if it wanted to end the conflict quickly, if it was anxious for a fight, if it was not concerned about maximum possible losses to its side, then the siege was not the appropriate strategy. For while sieges were effective, they did not bring victory overnight.

Some battles and wars in life can be fought by direct assault, and we can behold victory immediately. However, more often than not the great battles of our lives are won through sieges. Most of the warfare that we face is protracted and will require patience, endurance, vigilance, faithfulness, watching, and waiting on our part. Ofttimes we look at difficult situations and, if we can't come up with an immediate solution, we give up and declare that victory is impossible. Before giving up, however, perhaps we ought to submit some situations and persons to a "prayer-and-faith siege."

If there is a difficult person in your life and direct assaults are not working—if talking, arguing, crying, pleading, and even trying to set a good example are not working—put that person under a prayer-and-faith siege. Submit that unruly son or daughter, that husband or wife who won't do right to a prayer-and-faith siege. The more such persons act up, the harder you pray. Don't let their conduct wear down your faith; rather let your prayers wear *them* out. If you have a weakness, submit it to a prayer-and-faith siege. The more the Adversary attacks, the harder you pray. Don't let the attacks of the Adversary stop you from praying because you lose a few battles in the midst of your warfare. Remember, all the demons in hell tremble when the weakest Christian prays from the heart. Remember, prayer strengthens us as it fights off the enemy. Don't let the devil's attacks wear you down; rather *you* wear the devil down through your prayer.

Commit whatever and whomever you have in your life and can't handle to the Lord, and ask God to do what you can't. If we fight with prayer and faith, if we pray not for our will but God's, then victory is ours. We must, however, have faith to continue in prayer and believe in victory even during those times when nothing seems to be happening.

Syria's siege against Samaria was effective. Within the city an unsavory, unwholesome, and ceremonially unclean donkey's head was sold for twenty-eight dollars for food, while a pint of dove's dung went for three dollars. There were even reports of mothers who had boiled their children and eaten them. It was then, when the famine was most severe, when the spirits and morale of the people of Israel were at their lowest, when the city of Samaria was on the verge of collapse and anarchy and the victory of the Syrians seemed certain, when no one seemed able to do anything to stop Samaria's demise, when defeat was a matter of days or even hours away—it was at such a time that the prophet Elisha appeared before the king.

Elisha came in the twilight of a closing day, as the evening shadows began to lengthen and thicken over a city already engulfed in gloom, and made a startling prediction. Elisha said, "Hear the word of the Lord: thus says the Lord, by this time tomorrow grain shall be in such abundant supply that at the very gate of Samaria, wheat will be sold for a dollar and fifty cents a bushel, and barley for seventy-five cents a bushel" (see 2 Kings 7:1).

Can we imagine how a preacher or anyone else would be perceived in our day if he or she appeared on the six o'clock news on Wednesday and declared in the name of the Lord that, by the time of the evening news on Thursday, poverty and racism would disappear from America, or apartheid would vanish overnight in South Africa, or that tensions in the Middle East would suddenly go away and wars would cease to be? If some of us had been present when Elisha made his prediction, we would have asked, along with the king's captain or right-hand man, "If the LORD himself should make windows in heaven"—and cause it to rain down wheat and barley—"could this thing be?" (2 Kings 7:2). Yet as illogical and as impossible as the promises and predictions of God's Word may sound, we must be careful about disbelieving and doubting, mocking and making light of them.

Consider an old man approaching a hundred years old and his wife, who is approaching ninety, being told, "By this time next year, you shall bear a son." "If the LORD himself should make windows in heaven, could this thing be?" Yet according to the promise of the Lord's angel, Isaac was born in the following year (see Genesis 21:1-7). Watch Jesus approach Martha, whose brother had been dead for four days, whose body had been entombed, and, according to the normal cycle of nature, should have been in the process of decomposition. Hear Jesus tell this heartbroken sister that her brother would live again. Martha said to him, "I know that he will rise again in the resurrection at the last day." But Jesus said to her, "I am the resurrection and the life, and whoever lives and believes in me shall never die." See Jesus as he stands at the entrance of the tomb and calls Lazarus by name. See Lazarus come forth bound in the funeral wrappings of death. Hear Jesus command, "Unbind him, and let him go" (see John 11:1-44). "If the LORD himself should make windows in heaven, could this thing be?"

Everyone knows that when we give, we end up with less, not more. If we have ten apples and give one away, we end up with nine, not fifteen. Yet Jesus tells us, "Give, and it will be given to you; good measure, pressed down, shaken together, running over, will be put into your lap" (Luke 6:38). "If the LORD himself should make windows in heaven, could this thing be?"

How can we ever forget the incident that occurred in the ministry of Elisha's predecessor, Elijah, and the widow of Zarephath? In another time of famine, Elijah was led of the Spirit of God to ask a widow with a son to make him a cake of bread with her last meal in the barrel and her last cooking oil, with the promise that she would not go lacking. The widow scraped the bottom of the barrel and used her last meal and oil by faith in the words of the man of God. When she went back to the barrel and shook the cruse of oil, not only had what she used been replenished; it had been increased. For the three years that Elijah dwelt in her house, the meal was not spent from the barrel, and the oil did not run out of the cruse. "If the LORD himself should make windows in heaven, could this thing be?"

As incredible as Elisha's prophecy was, yet it may have been more palatable or believable if the prophet had revealed how it would come about. Elisha may not have known himself when he delivered God's word. Ours is not to know how God will work things out; ours is to believe that, to paraphrase Paul, "Things will turn out just as we've been told." Ours is not to know God's plan of action but to believe God's Word. When we board an airplane, ours is not to ride in the cockpit with the navigator and the pilot. When we board a ship, ours is not to go to the bridge and help the captain steer it. When we board a train or a subway, we do not proceed to the engine to assist the engineer in steering. When we get on a bus, there is no seat beside the driver for us. When we get into a car, no matter how much we instruct the driver, only one person can apply the brakes, press the gas pedal, and turn the steering wheel. Whether we're on a plane, train, ship, bus, or car, we must occupy the space allotted for passengers and trust the conveyer of the vehicle to take us to our destination. As passengers of faith, it is not ours to question how God, the pilot of the universe, the captain of our salvation, the engineer of our destiny, and the driver of every heartbeat will fulfill his Word or keep his promises. Ours is to keep our hand in the hand of the One who rules the waters and calms the sea. We have not gone through all the chambers of God's storehouse; God's ways are not ours but are far beyond ours and past searching out. And God is still able to work in mysterious ways the wonders of a beneficent providence to perform.

"If the LORD himself should make windows in heaven, could this thing be?" Elisha answered, "You shall see [the abundance of grain] with your own eyes, but you shall not eat of it" (2 Kings 7:2). It was during this time when the famine was most severe, when Samaria seemed to be doomed and Syria appeared to be invincible, when the king of Israel and his forces seemed powerless and only the man of God offered any word of hope, that four lepers were seated outside the city gates contemplating their fate. As they sat there with starving kinsfolk behind them and their enemies all around them, they asked themselves a question: "Why do we sit here till we die? If we go into the city where there is famine, we shall die. If we sit and do nothing but complain and feel sorry for ourselves, we shall die. If we go over to the camp of the Syrians who are our enemies, they may kill us—but perchance they may also save us. So let us go over to the Syrians. If they spare our lives, we shall live, and if they kill us, we shall but die, which is going to happen anyway, whether we sit here or go into the city" (see vv. 3-4).

Thus in the twilight of a closing day, as the evening shadows began to lengthen and thicken over a city already engulfed in gloom, the four lepers left the gates of Samaria and headed for the camp of the Syrians. However, when they reached the enemy camp, no one was there. According to the Scriptures, they had fled for their lives because "the LORD had made the army of the Syrians hear the sound of chariots, and of horses, the sound of a great army, so that they said to one another, 'Behold, the king of Israel has hired against us the kings of the Hittites and the kings of Egypt to come upon us' " (vv. 6-7). As the lepers went from tent to tent, eating and drinking their fill and storing away the treasures they had found, they remembered their brothers and sisters who were still perishing with hunger in the city and didn't know they had been delivered. They didn't know that they would not starve. They didn't know that the

Lord had answered their prayers and taken care of their enemies. They didn't know that the Lord had already kept his promise. The lepers believed that they would lose their own blessing if they tried to keep what they found to themselves. So they went back to the city and told the king what they had found.

Salvation is not only rejoicing in the hope that is within us; it is also sharing the Good News with others about what God has already done for us. Those who are bound today need to know that they don't have to live in fear or in captivity, for the enemy has already been defeated; they just don't know it. No power in this life is supreme but God. Their souls have been delivered, and they don't know it. Victory over their weaknesses is right within their reach, and they don't know it. The only way they can find out is for someone who has experienced what God can do to testify about what he or she has personally learned about redemption.

People grow tired of hearing talk about giving and tithing. However, God will bless and take care of you if you believe and follow his Word and his promises, no matter how illogical or impossible they may seem. If you are worried about how you're going to make it from day to day, you need to hear the news that if you put God's will first in your life in everything—including your giving by faith in accordance with God's Word—then God will keep meal in your barrel and oil in your cruse.

When the four lepers told what they experienced in the Syrian camp, the king dispatched a small search party to see if what they were saying was true. When you speak the truth, you don't have to worry about persons investigating your story. You can tell them, "Come and see." Don't take my word about what God can do for you—come and see. Don't take my word about how God will take care of you if you tithe—come and see. The search party brought back the news that the story of the lepers was true. When people come and see for themselves, they discover the truth of God's deliverance and how God keeps promises.

The people of Samaria ran from the city to the camp of the Syrians and plundered it. Consequently, a bushel of wheat was sold in the city gates that day for a dollar and fifty cents and a bushel of barley for seventy-five cents. The king's captain, who asked despairingly, "If the LORD himself should make windows in heaven, could this thing be?" was put in charge of the city gate. Unfortunately, the people in their excitement knocked him down and trod him underfoot. Thus was fulfilled the word of Elisha: "You shall see it with your own eyes, but you shall not eat of it" (v. 2). Those who doubt, who harden their hearts and set their faces as flint to God's Word, don't stop the promise from being fulfilled; they only cut off their own blessings, their own growth, and their own enjoyment of a revealed and promised Word that has been fulfilled.

For God keeps promises. "God is not a human being, that he should lie, or a mortal, that he should change his mind. Has he promised, and will he not do it? Has he spoken, and will he not fulfill it?" (Numbers 23:19, NRSV). God keeps promises. "The Lord is not slack concerning his promise" (2 Peter 3:9, KJV). God keeps promises. "If the LORD himself should make windows in heaven, could this thing be?" We serve a God who is able and willing to open a window in heaven to keep a promise. Hear this promise: "Bring the full tithe into the storehouse, so that there may be food in my house, and thus put me to the test, says the LORD of hosts; see if I will not open the windows of heaven for you and pour down for you an overflowing blessing" (Malachi 3:10, NRSV).

13. How Can I Repay the Lord for All His Goodness to Me?

Psalm 116:1-19

The word *psalm,* as we know, means song. In the Hebrew Scriptures, the title of the writings that we know as "Psalms" is "Tillim" or "Sefir Tehillim," which means "praises" or "book of praises." When we read the book of Psalms, we are reading essentially the hymnbook of the Jewish faith. We are reading a praise book or a word hymnal that was meant to be sung, often with instrumental accompaniment, rather than merely recited. Although all of the psalms do not have praise as their central theme, Psalm (Song) 116 certainly does. From its opening words to its conclusion, it abounds with praise and thanksgiving.

One can only imagine the thrill of being in the assembly of worshiping Israelites as the soloist or choir, under the direction of the choirmaster and accompanied by the trumpet, harp, tambourine, cymbals, strings, and dancing, began to testify to God's goodness and mercy, God's delivering and way-making power and sang:

I love the LORD, for he heard my voice;
    he heard my cry for mercy.
Because he turned his ear to me,
    I will call on him as long as I live.

The cords of death entangled me,
    the anguish of the grave came upon me;
    I was overcome by trouble and sorrow.
Then I called on the name of the LORD:
    "O LORD, save me!" (Psalm 116:1-4, NIV).

85

Imagine with me now that you are hearing the playing of the harp and other stringed instruments as the soloist or choir continues to sing:

> The LORD is gracious and righteous;
> > our God is full of compassion.
> The LORD protects the simplehearted;
> > when I was in great need, he saved me.
>
> Be at rest once more, O my soul,
> > for the LORD has been good to you.
>
> For you, O LORD, have delivered my soul from death,
> > my eyes from tears,
> > my feet from stumbling,
> that I may walk before the LORD
> > in the land of the living (vv. 5-9, NIV).

Now the trumpets and the cymbals come in, while tears appear in the eyes of the singers as they reflect on the goodness of the Lord in their own lives and the stress that God's hand has delivered them from, the tight places that God's wisdom has guided them through, the physical pain and the sorrow that God's Spirit has comforted, and thus they raise their voices in unashamed, praiseworthy, and melodic emotion, asking in awe today's crucial question:

> How can I repay the LORD
> > for all his goodness to me?
> I will lift up the cup of salvation
> > and call on the name of the LORD.
> I will fulfill my vows to the LORD
> > in the presence of all his people. . . .
>
> I will sacrifice a thank offering to you
> > and call on the name of the LORD.
> I will fulfill my vows to the LORD
> > in the presence of all his people,
> in the courts of the house of the LORD—
> > in your midst, O Jerusalem (vv. 12-14, 17-18).

For a moment the music stops, every eye is on the choirmaster, who raises his or her hands, and together all the instruments sound, the liturgical dancers swirl in a circle, and both choir and congregation join together and sing one great "praise the Lord" or, to use the Hebrew expression, "hallelujah."

The question of giving is best asked, answered, and understood as an expression of thanksgiving and praise for the goodness of the Lord. To get the most personal fulfillment from giving, to know the full joy of giving, to be able to give as generously as we should, giving has to be seen as an expression of thanksgiving and praise for the goodness of the Lord. As each of us ponders whether we will begin (or continue) to tithe by faith—or how much of our time, talents, or treasures we're willing to give to the Lord through the work of the church—the crucial question we must ask ourselves is not just, "How much shall I give from what I have?" or "How much can I afford to give?" It's not just, "How much time from my busy schedule can I afford to give to the church? How much of my talent can I afford to give to the church without being compensated for my services? How much of my money (the Lord's money) would I be giving away if I tithed?" It's not, "Do you know how much I would be putting in if I tithed?"

Whenever I hear that question, I want to say, "Evidently the Lord is really blessing you. So instead of looking at the 10 percent you're giving away, perhaps you ought look at the 90 percent you're keeping and praise God that 10 percent is all that is being asked as a minimum." Instead of complaining about the 10 percent that's being asked, perhaps we ought to praise God for the 90 percent that's left. If our tithe is too much to give away, perhaps we ought to ask the Lord to reduce our totals so that when we tithe we would be giving far less away. Job serves as a reminder to all of us that the Lord gives and, but for the protection of almighty God, the devil can take it all away.

The crucial question that ought to direct our giving is not simply, "How much should I give?" but "How can I repay the Lord for all his goodness to me?" Unless our giving is motivated by gratitude and is an act of praise for what God has already done in our lives, then our giving may be motivated and accompanied by the wrong attitude. Once our giving is seen primarily as another bill or obligation and the Lord is looked upon as another creditor, then our spirit of giving as well as our giving itself will be off center. A man once explained to his pastor that he didn't tithe because he couldn't afford it—he had too many other bills. The pastor told him that his first debt was to God. The man replied, "Yeah, I know; but the Lord ain't pushing me like my other creditors." Because the Lord doesn't push us, the Lord tends to lose when we look on the Lord as another creditor. When some of us get into a tight financial bind, the first place—not the last, or the middle, or even the second place—but the first place we cut is our giving to the church. I'm not talking about the person who has to put off a pledge for a season that is above or beyond the regular tithe and offering because of an unexpected financial setback. I'm talking about the person who merely tips the Lord—gives God the leftovers and looks for any excuse to give less and do less than what he or she is already not doing.

Yet the Lord gives us the health and the strength, blesses us with a job and a mind to budget, so that the other creditors can be paid. Is it asking too much that we do right by God from whom all blessings flow? A number of us can testify that we've never missed anything or gone lacking anything because of what we've given to the church. Even when we put in our last, we didn't go lacking because the Lord made a way for us. We've never gone hungry or without clothes or without a shelter over our heads because of what we've given to the church. Our lights have never been turned out or telephone turned off because of what we've given to the Lord. If we fell behind, it was because we spent too much on what we put in our stomachs or on our backs or in the places where we went for entertainment or because we were trying to keep up with the Joneses or trying to maintain the image of a certain lifestyle. What we've given at church was not the reason for our lack but the reason for our making it. For the Lord takes care of us even as we give. Thus our tithes and offerings, our pledges and sacrifices should not be viewed as bills but as gifts of praise and thanksgiving in response to what God has already done.

"How can I repay the LORD for all his goodness to me?" Or, as the Revised Standard Version puts it, "What shall I render to the LORD for all his bounty to me?" (Psalm 116:12). When I think about the journey over which I have come, I say to myself, "Look where God brought me from—from nothing to something, from nobody to somebody, from sinner to saint, from damnation to salvation, from sickbed to health, from death's door to new life, from no confidence to self-confidence, from dirt roads to paved boulevards, from walking to driving, from driving to flying, from mules to Mercedes, from the back of the bus to the front of the bus to the driver of the bus to the owner of the bus company, from slave ships to cruise ships, from cotton stockings to nylons, from overalls to silk suits, from being flat broke to money in the bank, from the basement to one of the top floors, from anything will do to nothing but the best, from places I'd heard and read about to places I've seen and visited that I didn't think I ever would see with my own eyes, from being called darkie to colored to nigger to nigra to Negro to black to African American, from ignorance to education, from a one-room school to a college or university, from being called boy and girl or auntie or uncle to young man or young woman or Mr. or Mrs. or Miss or Ms., from sharecropping to my own vine and fig tree, from cotton fields to big city mayors, from plantations to governors and congresspersons and senators, from shacks and cold-water flats to the steps of the White House.

From Freeborn Garretson to Martin Luther King Jr.; from Hiram Revels to William Gray; from Harriet Tubman to Eleanor Holmes Norton; from Crispus Attucks to Colin Powell; from P. B. S. Pinchback to Douglass Wilder; from Henry McNeal Turner to Jesse Jackson; from Phyllis Wheatley to Cicely Tyson; from Sojourner Truth to Shirley Chisholm; from Jarena Lee to Leontyne C. Kelly; from Paul Robeson to David Peaston.

We know that the journey ahead is filled with perils and that we have a long way to go before we reach freedom. But when some of us look back and see where we started from, there is a crucial question we must ask ourselves: "How can I repay the LORD for all his goodness to me?" Of course we know that ultimately we can never repay the Lord any more than we can repay a mother—or those who cared for us like a mother—for love that comforted us when we were sad, that stayed up with us when we were sick, who's tender hands wiped tears from our eyes, who guided us when we had questions, who gave us back our confidence when a mean devil and a racist society had shaken it, who prayed for us while we slept, and whose songs of faith calmed our fears and whose love taught us the meaning of love. We know that we can never repay the Lord any more than we can repay a father—or those who cared for us like a father—who worked long and hard to provide as best they could for us, who put themselves and their needs last in order that we might have, who kept all that they bore and felt to themselves in order that we might be at peace.

We know that we can no more repay God than we can true friends who stand by us through difficult days and lonely hours; who do without our asking and give without expecting to be repaid; who demand the best in us, from us, and out of us; who love us enough to tell us the truth. When we think about the goodness of the Lord, we're like the writer:

Were the whole realm of nature mine,
That were a present far too small:
Love so amazing, so divine,
Demands my soul, my life, my all.[1]

We know that we can never repay the Lord for his goodness and love, but we can and ought do something to express our gratitude. The psalmist answered the question, "How can I repay the LORD for all his goodness to me?" by saying, "I will lift up the cup of salvation and call on the name of the LORD."

Commentators have interpreted these words in various ways. Some have said that to acknowledge God's salvation in your life is to give yourself over to the glory of God. It is to understand that you live not for the glory of self but for the glory of God, that men and women, boys and girls may see the effects of God's saving grace in you and declare, "Look what the Lord has wrought." We respond to God's goodness by living for the God who saved us. Other commentators believe that the cup was part of a fellowship or festal meal, as found in Leviticus 7:11-21, that celebrated God's deliverance from sickness, trouble, or death or that acknowledged a special blessing. This meal was climaxed with a thank offering. Thus the psalmist wrote, "I will sacrifice a thank offering to you / and call on the name of the LORD. / I will fulfill my vows to the LORD / in the presence of all his people" (vv. 17-18).

Close to twenty years ago the African Methodist Episcopal Church—like a number of other churches and organizations and even a national government such as our own from time to time—was experiencing a financial crisis. In order to assist our church out of its difficulty, the bishops as leaders of the church set the example and made pledges toward the liquidation of the deficit. Bishop Isaiah Hamilton Bonner, who was one of the oldest bishops of the church (facing retirement at the next general conference), pledged more than anybody else. When asked why he pledged such a huge amount, he replied that he was making a thank offering. The Lord and the church had been good to him. The Lord had granted him a long life with a reasonable portion of health and strength and a sound mind. When a number of other bishops had been retired, the church had allowed him to remain in active service. Therefore, he was making a thank offering.

We would do well to see our giving not as another bill that we dread paying but as a thank offering that we gladly pay. For if God hadn't provided, I wouldn't be able to give. When I sing in the choir, that's part of my thank offering to God for giving me a voice and speech. When I stand at the door and usher, that's part of my thank offering to God for blessing me with health and strength. When I'm cooking in the kitchen or working around the church, that's part of my thank offering for God being so good to me. When I teach Sunday school, that's part of my thank offering for God giving me an understanding and love for his Word. When I'm feeding the hungry, visiting the sick, and doing missionary work, that's part of my thank offering. For I serve God by serving others. When I shout and rejoice, that's part of my thank and praise offering. When I preach God's Word, that's part of my thank offering for God's finding a way to use my meager talents. When I live for the Lord, that's my thank offering for Jesus saving my soul on Calvary.

1. Isaac Watts, "When I Survey the Wondrous Cross."

14. What Do Ye More than Others?

Matthew 5:43-48

"What do ye more than others?" This biting question is a call for introspection. "What do ye more than others?" asks Jesus. This insightful inquiry forces us to rip away all pretension and see ourselves as we really are. "What do ye more than others?" Let's think about that question if we dare. The question is not what the preacher or the church officers or other members do through or with their religion. The question is not what my neighbors, family members, or friends do in or by their religion. Questions about the commitment, sincerity, faith, and righteousness of others are some of the easiest to debate, discuss, and face. The question I would ask you to think about is this: "What do *ye* more than others?"

What is there that is distinctive about my living, loving, and giving that separates me from others who do not profess to be Christian? When people see me on my job, is there anything about me—about my language, my personality, the way I carry myself— that informs them that I am a Christian? Can people see any glow of joy, peace, niceness, character, trustworthiness, or style in me that lets them know that I have been bought with a price, that I am no longer my own, and that I am living for the One who loved me enough to redeem me? When I return home from church, can the people with whom I live see any difference, or am I as evil, disagreeable, and difficult to live with as I was before? Are there any positive changes in my attitude around the house that can be directly traced to the influence of my faith? When I walk across the school yard or sit in a classroom, is there anything distinctive about me as a young Christian?

What do I do that expresses who I am as God's child and what I

92

represent in terms of a godly moral code, without my having to constantly tell people? If we have to constantly tell people who we are, something is wrong. If you don't receive the respect due a lady, if you constantly have to remind people that you're a lady and should be respected as such, something is wrong. Evidently you're not acting like a lady! If we must constantly remind people that we are church officers, preachers, parents, adults, husbands, or wives, something is wrong. Evidently we are not acting like we should. People who carry themselves in a respectable way receive respect. People who carry themselves in a loving way receive love. What do we more than others that informs a skeptical, onlooking world that we are in fact what we claim to be in speech?

"What do I more than others?" When my patience wears thin and I am pushed beyond my breaking point and lose my temper, do I act any differently than others? Is there any more restraint of words or actions? When trouble erupts in my life, when trials and problems knock on my door, is there anything distinctive about the way I bear my burdens, face my stress, and handle my conflict? When sickness attacks my body, is there anything identifiably and distinctively different in my attitude regarding my affliction or the way I endure my own personal suffering? When disappointments come, is there anything different about the way I meet them and handle my frustrations? When failure haunts me, do I show any greater determination to snatch victory from the jaws of defeat? When I face overwhelming odds, do I show a greater faith to accomplish the impossible because I know that if God is for me, then God is more than the whole world against me? When death removes a loved one, do I mourn as one without hope of another day of greeting where there will be no more good-byes?

When faith is required, how much faith do we demonstrate? More than others? When vision is required, how much vision do we demonstrate? More than others? When forgiveness is required, how much forgiveness do we demonstrate? More than others? When tolerance for the differences of others and patience with the weaknesses and faults of others is required, how much tolerance and patience do we demonstrate? More than others? When love is required, how much love do we demonstrate? More than others?

How different are our thoughts from others'? How different are the desires of our hearts from others'? In a money-hungry, money-grabbing, money-worshiping world, how different are our attitudes regarding money from others'? In a society that has come to believe that gadgetry is the measure of all things and that life really does consist in the abundance of possessions, how different is our attitude toward material possessions from others'? Or are we Christians also caught in the illusive trap of substituting quality of life and character with a quantity of things? How different is our attitude regarding status and the use of power from others'? In a world of selfishness, how different is our sense of altruism and praxis of sacrifice from others'? What do ye—what do I—more than others?

There are times when we believe that we are displaying Christian virtue when we are only demonstrating ordinary human character. We are nice to those who are nice to us. We remember the hands that helped us and the feet that kicked us. We are more than willing to extend ourselves to those who helped us, and the only time some of us show real patience is when we "bide our time" until we can get back at those who kicked us. When we've returned a kindness with a kindness, we feel as if we've manifested some great Christian virtue—after all, we're not ingrates.

Well, according to Jesus, loving our friends is no great achievement. Anybody, whether Christian or not, can do that. Being nice to those who are nice to us is no great Christian act of benevolence; anyone has sense enough to be nice to those who are nice to them. Good politics returns favor for favor. Even a dog has sense enough not to bite the hand that feeds it.

We're not being great Christians just because we love our families and take care of them. A lot of people who love and take care of their families are still going to hell. Racist white people love their families. The concept of family is important in organized crime; leaders of organized crime are known to be devoted to their families. Many merchants of sex exploitation love their families; they won't allow their own families to be exposed to the filth that they market to others. Drug dealers love their families; they wouldn't dare feed their families the poison that they give to others. Being a responsible family member is noble, and I believe that it is unchristian not to take care of our family responsibilities, but loving one's family is not a distinctively Christian virtue as such. Anyone can love family. "What do ye more than others?"

In a racist world anyone can love his or her own kind. In a world that denigrates and oppresses rather than celebrates and respects the racial, cultural, and political differences among people, anyone can salute his or her brothers and sisters only. Not much leadership is required to exploit feelings of hostility, distrust, and fear between races. Anyone can keep people with a history of division and misunderstanding divided. In an era of increasing racial polarization, Jesus has a question for those of us who are called by his name: "What do ye more than others?"

Jesus calls us to the extraordinary; he calls us to go beyond the minimum. He challenges us to go farther and do more than others. Thus he says to us in the words of our text:

> Ye have heard that it hath been said, Thou shalt love thy neighbour, and hate thine enemy. But I say unto you, Love your enemies, bless them that curse you, do good to them that hate you, and pray for them which despitefully use you, and persecute you; That ye may be the children of your Father which is in heaven: for he maketh his sun to rise on the evil and on the good, and sendeth rain on the just and on the unjust. For if ye love them which love you, what reward have ye? do not even the publicans the same? And if ye salute your brethren only, what do ye more than others? do not even the publicans so? Be ye therefore perfect [in love], even as your Father which is in heaven is perfect (Matthew 5:43-48, KJV).

What do ye more than others in loving? What do ye more than others in giving? As we are called to be extraordinary livers and lovers, we are also called to be extraordinary givers. One cannot love without giving. Giving is as basic and integral to our faith as loving is. As heat is basic to fire, wetness to water, darkness to night, and light to day, so is giving basic to our faith. As breathing is basic to living, so is giving. As one cannot be a Christian without loving, neither can one be a Christian without giving.

Sometimes people say, "I get so tired of coming to church to hear the preacher beg." (Whenever the church or the preacher mentions money, some people consider that to be begging.) "I get so tired of hearing all this talk about money, tithing, and giving. When I come to church, I don't come to hear about money. I come to hear the gospel preached." People who make such statements don't know their Bible. Omit every reference to money in the life of Jesus, and there would not be much of a gospel left. After all, gold was brought at his birth, and a treasurer had to be appointed to handle the contributions that people gave to our Lord. He was questioned about his payment of the temple tax and asked if taxes should be paid to Caesar. He was asked to intercede in the case of one brother who would not divide the family inheritance with another brother. He had to deal with money changers in the temple. Thirty pieces of silver was the price on his head. Take out the references to money and giving, and we would not have the narrative of the widow's mite, Zacchaeus's conversion, the rich young ruler seeking eternal life, and the anointing at Bethany with expensive oil.

Author Charles Shedd writes, "One verse out of every six in Matthew, Mark and Luke deals specifically with a man and his possessions. Nearly one-third of those marvelous parables which Christ told focus on this theme."[1] Take out every reference to money, our possessions, and giving, and there would be no parable of the householder with treasures old and new, no parable of the pearl of great price, no parable about counting the cost before building. There would be no parable of the two debtors, no parable of the unmerciful servant, no parable of the unjust steward, no parable of the rich fool. There would be no parable of the talents and the pounds, no parable of the good Samaritan, no parable of the lost coin, and no parable of the prodigal son. People who want to hear the gospel need to understand that when we talk about money and about our attitudes toward our possessions, giving, and tithing, we are preaching the gospel. It may not be the gospel they want to hear, but it is the gospel of our Lord and Savior Jesus Christ.

I repeat, giving is at the center of our faith, and it is impossible to be a Christian without giving. As surely as we must be born again to enter the kingdom of heaven, we must give. As surely as we must bear a cross, we must give. As surely as we must forgive, we must give. As surely as we must preach or witness to the Word, we must give. As surely as we must breathe, we must give.

For us, to give is to live. Everything that lives gives. Not to give is a sign of death. Dead flowers give no fresh fragrance. Dead people don't give—and if we've ever received anything from anyone who has passed away, she or he made the provision to give it when still alive. People who try to hold on to everything may have hearts and pulses that beat, but inside they are dead. When we read the story of Ebenezer Scrooge in Charles Dickens's *A Christmas Carol,* we discover that Scrooge came to life and really started living only when he started giving. In George Eliot's story of *Silas Marner,* the old miser started enjoying life only when he started to give.

You may know of the comparison between the two great bodies of water in ancient Palestine. One body of water has no inlets or outlets; it retains all of its water, receiving nothing from any other body and giving nothing to any other body. No boats sail across its surface, no fish swim in its depths, no children play along its shore. It is never mentioned in the Gospels; Jesus is never recorded as going there. It is known as the Dead Sea. The other body of water gives and receives from other tributaries. For centuries its water was the mainstay of the fishing industry for that region. Along its shores children play, and across its surface boats sail. We read of its influence throughout the Gospels, for Jesus visited there many times. It is known as the Sea of Galilee. To give is to live.

Jesus described himself as the bread of life, the light of the world, the door, the good shepherd, and the true vine—all of which give. Bread gives itself to be eaten, light gives itself to chase away the darkness, the door opens to green pastures, the shepherd gives himself to the sheep, and the vine gives itself to the grape. Bread that is not eaten becomes stale; light that is not given becomes midnight; hinges rust on doors that are not opened; shepherds who do not give become hirelings; a vine that does not give becomes useless. We have a Savior who gives. "What do we more than others?"

God made the sun—it gives.
God made the moon—it gives.
God made the star—it gives.
God made the air—it gives.
God made the clouds—they give.
[God made heaven—it gives.]
God made the earth—it gives.
God made the sea—it gives.
God made the trees—they give.
God made the flowers—they give.
God made the plants—they give.
God made the birds—they give.
God made the beasts—they give.

God made man—he . . .[2]
God made woman—she . . .
God made human beings—they . . .
"What do ye more than others?"

1. Charles Shedd, *How to Develop a Tithing Church* (Nashville: Abingdon, 1961), 76.
2. "God Made the Sun," from Paul Lee Tan, *Encyclopedia of 7700 Illustrations*, (Garland: Assurance Publishers, 1979), 473.

15. The Burden of Our Blessings

Luke 12:48b

This text, drawn from the parable that teaches us to be ever vigilant and ready for the Lord's coming, also establishes the principles of accountability and responsibility. Blessings are not to be treated as pearls placed before swine—unappreciated, mismanaged, mistreated, trampled upon, and abused. We are not to do with our blessings whatever we please—as if they are ours. Blessings are given to us to manage, for the Bible teaches us that God, the giver of every good and perfect gift, holds us accountable for the way we treat the blessings that heaven's grace bestows upon our lives. However we're blessed—whether with riches, education, a good job, a good companion, children, the exuberance of youth, long life, friends or people who love us, health, a creative mind, a particular talent or talents, or spirituality—we must manage our blessings wisely and handle them well. For one day we shall give an account for the way we have treated or mistreated our blessings. As our text informs us, "From everyone to whom much has been given, much will be required; and from the one to whom much has been entrusted, even more will be demanded" (Luke 12:48b, NRSV).

Our text not only reminds us of the burden for accountability and responsibility of our blessings; I believe it also teaches us about God's expectations of our giving. God is extremely fair; God expects us to give only what we have. If we have much, God expects much, and if we have little, God expects a fair measure of devotion from our little. God doesn't expect a person who doesn't have a job or who is on public assistance to give the same amount as the person whose income is in the six-figure bracket. God does not expect a child on an allowance to give the same amount as his or her working parent. But God does expect that child to be taught to give something from what he or she has.

God is unlike anyone else to whom we will ever give. When we run up our light bill, we pay what the utility company demands. The utility company doesn't look at how much we have and say to us, "Give as you've been blessed. If you have much, then pay much, or if you have little, then donate little." The utility company says, "This is what you owe; pay for what you used. Pay it or out go your lights." The same principle applies at the grocery store. You pay for what you get. Whether by cash or check or food stamps, you pay for what you get. Both the wealthy and those on welfare who shop in the same store will pay the same price.

However, God requires only that we be fair and give as we have been blessed. "From everyone to whom much has been given, much will be required; and from the one to whom much has been entrusted, even more will be demanded." Most of us understand and accept this principle. Yet as fair as it is, it rises or falls on our understanding of one word—*much*. Most of us will gladly testify that God is good—all the time—and that we have been blessed—until it comes to the issue of our giving. At this point we stop talking about how much we've been blessed and start crying about how much we owe on our bills. We say, "True, I've been blessed but—I've got a mortgage," or "my rent keeps going up"; "but my child in school"; "but I'm supporting several of my family members"; "but I'm on fixed income"; "but I'm not well and my medicine is so expensive"; "but the cost of living keeps going up"; "but I've got to get a new coat"; "but my car keeps acting up"; "but the prices at the grocery store seem to go up every time I go there." "True, I've been blessed, but when I look at all I have to pay out, I don't have much left. True, from everyone to whom much is given, much is required, but that doesn't apply to me. That applies to my employer or Doctor So-and-So, Mr. John Doe, or old widow What's-her-name (whose husband left her well-off). If I had their money, I would give much more, but when I look at my obligations, I don't have much to give."

One of the things we forget about is that the term *much* is relative. What is little to us looks like much to a lot of other people. If you don't believe me, ask the victims of any hurricane, fire, and flood who have lost everything. Ask people in Russia who must stand in unbelievably long lines to buy the necessities of life. While we complain about prices at the grocery store, the people of Somalia would be thrilled just to stand in our grocery line. Ask the people of Liberia and Haiti what they think about our little. Many of our parents and grandparents would have thought that heaven had come to earth if they had some of our little.

Luke 18:18-30, along with the other Synoptic Gospels (Matthew and Mark), tells the story of a rich young ruler who came to Jesus asking, "What must I do to inherit eternal life?" We have all criticized this young man for letting his riches block his way to the Kingdom. And some of us have self-righteously declared that if we had had his riches, our response would have been different. Well, I don't know how rich he was, but this I know: he never rode in a car, turned on a light, heard a piano or pipe organ, watched a television or heard a radio, rode in an airplane or on a train, slept on an inner-spring mattress, talked on a telephone, saw a typewritten letter or a calculator or computer. He never checked a book out of a library or improved his vision with a pair of eyeglasses or his hearing with a hearing aid. He never saw water running out of a faucet or used a washing machine or dryer or garbage disposal or dishwasher or even a commode. And if he was rich, what are we?[1] Hear the Word of the Lord: "From everyone from whom much has been given, much will be required; and from the one to whom much has been entrusted, even more will be demanded."

A small boy asked his father for money for the church offering. The father said he had only a penny in change. (That's our first mistake, parents. We give our children dollars for the movies, and dollars for pizzas, and only change for the church offering and Sunday school.) But the boy replied, "I can't put just a penny in the collection." The father asked, "Why not?" The boy said, "You don't want me to look cheap to the Lord, do you?"[2] When we look at how we've been blessed—food that goes bad in our refrigerators, clothes that hang in our closets that we don't wear, can't wear, and won't give away—how does what we put in the church offering look to the Lord? When we look at the money we smoke up, drink up, and use to make ourselves look better and smell better; when we look at the money we invest in the lottery, in the numbers, at the racetrack, in one-armed bandits, and in little things we just enjoy doing and having—in spite of all our other bills—how does what we put in the church offering look to the Lord?

When we think about the fact that every day God gives us health and strength to do whatever we need to do that day; every day in ways that we can't number God shows his steadfast love, perpetual care, and never-failing protection of us, how does what we give at church look to the Lord? God so loved us that God gave his only begotten Son, Jesus Christ, for our redemption. God so loved us that he hung him high and stretched him wide, that we might be saved—that upon his return to glory that we would have a Comforter, the Holy Spirit, to guide us into the truth and empower us for living. The Comforter came as promised on the day of Pentecost, with gifts and new life for believers. Even now Jesus Christ lives to intercede for us at the mercy seat and is coming back to reward his faithful servants. We celebrate the fact that death no longer has dominion over us and that nothing has to keep us in bondage, but in Jesus Christ we have cleansing for our sins, peace in the midst of our trouble, joy on our journey, the resurrection from the dead, and hope of eternal glory. When we think about all this, how does what we give in church look to the Lord? Hear the Word of the Lord, "From everyone to whom much is given, much will be required." When God has been so good to us, we dare not look cheap to the Lord.

Giving, however, is not simply a matter of money. We've been blessed, and we have received much in many ways other than material blessings. The parable in Matthew 18:23-35 teaches us of the unforgiving servant. If we have been forgiven, then we ought to give some forgiveness to others. If God has been patient with us—with our broken promises, good intentions that never got off the ground, and vows made in earnest when we were in trouble and forgotten in callousness after we had been delivered—then we ought to be patient with the faults and failings of others. We ought not be so quick to give up on people and send them to hell. I'm so glad that God who is perfect is not as quick to send people to hell as we imperfect, self-righteous humans, who are barely escaping it ourselves. I know sometimes when we see people who have wronged us, we ask ourselves why we should forgive them, particularly when they don't show any signs of change or repentance. We forgive because we have been forgiven. We forgive because we have been told, "Though your sins be as scarlet, they shall be as white as snow" (Isaiah 1:18, KJV). We forgive because we have had to pray:

"Have mercy on me, O God, according to your steadfast love; according to your abundant mercy blot out my transgressions" (Psalm 51:1, NRSV). We forgive because Jesus prayed on our behalf, "Father, forgive them; for they do not know what they are doing" (Luke 23:34, NRSV). "From everyone to whom much is given, much will be required."

Giving is also a matter of service. Mark 1:30-31 tells the story of Jesus' healing Peter's mother-in-law. When the fever left her, she began to serve them. She not only shouted; she served. She not only testified, she served. She not only said thank you, she served. If God has done something special for you, if God has healed, delivered, made a way out of no way, worked a miracle, answered a heartfelt prayer, brought the wandering feet of a loved one back home, helped you get over a heartache, given you strength to pick up broken pieces of your heart and live and love anew—then you ought not be stingy with your service. We ought to be willing to serve however we can, wherever we can, whenever we can—with a glad mind and a willing spirit. Nobody ought to have to beg us to serve; we ought to do it for the simple reason that God is good—all the time. If there's something we can do, we shouldn't wait to be asked; we ought to step forward and volunteer, for the sole reason that God is good—all the time. If we are never recognized or our names are never called, that's all right. We're not serving for recognition or even for future rewards; we're serving because God has been good and is still good—all the time. And if others want to talk about us and falsely accuse us, we're not going to allow idle talk from idle minds with empty hearts and busybody spirits stop us from serving a God who is good—all the time. How we feel about the preacher isn't even important. What is important is that we render service to a God who is good—all the time. In trouble and trials, sickness and sorrow, through problems and pain, God is good—all the time. That's why we're singing in the choir, ushering at the door, taking abuse as a leader, making sacrifice as a member, meeting late at night on special projects, cooking in the kitchen, volunteering in the office, taking time with the young, caring for the sick, strengthening the faith of the discouraged—because God has been good to us, and God's Word tells us, "From everyone to whom much has been given, much will be required; and from the one to whom much has been entrusted, even more will be demanded."

As a minimum standard of our giving in return for what God has done for us, the Bible talks about a tithe, a consecrated 10 percent, as a starting point of our thanksgiving. Ten percent of our time, talent, and treasure. In terms of time that's only six minutes out of every hour, two hours and twenty-four minutes of every day, almost seventeen hours every week. Ten percent ought to be our starting point. In terms of talent that's 10 percent of our cooking, cleaning, singing, talking, typing, writing, teaching, decorating, counseling, transacting, painting that ought be our starting point of service to God, God's church, and God's people. In terms of our money, 10 percent of our income—salary or whatever income we have—off the top, ought be our minimum financial gift to God. And if we say, "That's a lot," remember that God has blessed "a lot"; God has answered prayers "a lot"; God has forgiven "a lot"; God has loved "a lot"; God has been good "a lot." When we were in sin, God saved "a lot." God has provided "a lot"; God has protected "a lot." When we were empty, God filled us "a lot." When we were down, God raised us "a lot." When we were sick, God healed us "a lot." When we were bound, God delivered "a lot." "From everyone to whom much is given, much will be required; and from the one to whom much has been entrusted, even more will be demanded."

1. Robert L. Shannon and Michael J. Shannon, *Stewardship Source Book* (Cincinnati: Standard Publishing, 1987), 85.
2. R. L. Speaks, *God in an Age of Scarcity* (Charlotte: A.M.E. Publishing House, 1981), 82.

16. "It Just Don't Make No Sense"

Luke 6:38

A character from Melvin Van Peeple's play *Ain't Supposed to Die a Natural Death* talks about how everything the African American male does is suspect. He concludes by saying, "It just don't make no sense. If I stand, I'm loitering; if I walk, I'm prowling; if I run, I'm escaping; if I sit, I'm shiftless; (if I act like I want to get up on my feet, I'm ambitious;) if I frown, I'm hostile; if I smile, I'm Uncle Tom; if I look tired, I'm on junk; if I stumble, I'm drunk; if I wash, I'm a pimp; if I don't, I'm a bum."[1] It just don't make no sense.

At first glance the words of our text don't make no sense either. Everyone knows that when you pay something out or give something away, you end up with less, not more. If you have two apples and give one away, you end up with one apple, not three. If you have ten pennies and give one away, you end up with nine pennies, not fifteen. If you have one dollar and give that away, you end up with nothing, not two dollars. Subtraction always means less; it does not mean multiplication or addition. Yet our text tells us, "Give and it will be given to you; good measure, pressed down, shaken together, running over, will be put into your lap" (Luke 6:38). It just don't make no sense.

The statement isn't logical, and as humans we are a logical species. Of course I'm always amazed at the illogical things that this logical species does—things that truly just don't make no sense. All around us we see the results of smoking, drinking, overeating, and drugs, and yet we continue to experiment with these things, things that have been proven to be hazardous to our health—it just don't make no sense. We read the Bible and biographies of various

105

people and we see what has happened to persons who did certain things, lived a certain lifestyle, and had certain attitudes. Logically we should look at them, learn from their mistakes or examples, and shape our lives thereby. Yet we persist in doing the things they've done that have led to their destruction, stumbling, and falling, as if the same things won't happen to us— it just don't make no sense.

We know that we have the means to destroy each other, and yet the nations of this world still try to settle disputes by the barrel of a gun. We know what we are doing to the earth, yet we still continue to destroy it. After centuries and centuries of disputes, the Middle East is still a powder keg of the world, as generation after generation is fueled with the same venom. A white minority in South Africa believed that it could keep the black majority down forever— it just don't make no sense. It just don't make no sense to have homelessness in America when we are smart enough and rich enough to put people on the moon. It don't make no sense to have hungry people in America or anywhere else in the world when we're paying farmers not to grow food.

Of course, there are many other things that don't make no sense either. In a highly scientific, technological, computerized age, love that cannot be either seen or measured still makes the world go 'round. In spite of skyrocketing divorce rates and failed marriages all around them, people still grow into love and marry—and some of them make it, despite the odds against them. Some of those who were not supposed to make it, who had most things going against them, made it. And some of those who had most things going for them, didn't; it just don't make no sense.

The same is true for individuals as well as couples and relationships. Look at any graduating class twenty years later, or a group of childhood friends who have became adults. Some who were supposed to do well, who seemed destined for the top, have fallen far short of everybody's expectations—while others considered to be average or bound for failure have surprised everyone with the things they've done with their lives and the kinds of persons they've turned out to be. It just don't make no sense. Stones that builders reject becoming cornerstones—it makes no sense.

Faith that continues to believe even when everything around it contradicts it; hope that looks at the blackest of nights and sees a new day coming; dedication that keeps on keeping on even when it is being kicked in the teeth—these make no sense.

There is much in life that "just don't make no sense." That's why we must be careful about doubting God's Word—because it's not always logical. We must always be careful about trying to make our religion or all that we believe logical. God is not bound by our logic, by our notions of what makes sense. It's not that God is antilogical, or that religion and faith are anti-intellectual or antiacademic. God is the creator of human intelligence and logic. God is not the creator of sin and evil, of ignorance and stupidity. God is the creator of intelligence and logic; God's enterprises, religion and faith, are not anti-intellectual, antiacademic, antieducational, or antiscientific. God is simply supralogical—above logic. Isaiah records the Lord as saying, "My thoughts are not your thoughts, nor are your ways my ways" (55:8, NRSV). Religion and faith, then, are not antiacademic or antiscientific, although they sometimes deal in truth that cannot be found in books or verified in scientific laboratories. However, their truths can be experienced in life and are verified in eternity.

This statement of Jesus makes no sense; it isn't logical, but it's true nevertheless. It's true because God will always find a way to confirm his Word. Sometimes we say, "I know somebody who gives all the time, and she is still poor. I don't see where God is blessing her in abundance." Never forget that God has more than one way to bless. Sometimes we take the verse to mean that if we give ten dollars, God will bless us with twenty or thirty dollars. Sometimes God may bless that way, but never believe that the abundant, pressed down, shaken together, and overflowing blessing of God as a response to giving and sacrifice can come only in the form of more money, or a new car, or a new house.

I enjoy hearing tithing testimonies of those who say that since they've been tithing, they have more money, a better job, and so on. Money and material things are not the total blessing, however, or the only way God can bless your life. Having health and strength to enjoy what you have—and sense enough to appreciate it—that's also part of the blessing. Being more pleasant and agreeable, more humble in spirit and more grateful in heart—that's also part of the blessing. Being able to enjoy and praise God for however you are blessed—that's also part of the blessing. For when giving is done with the right attitude and spirit, we become more sensitive to the goodness of God in our lives.

We realize that even after we've sacrificed, God is still so much better to us than we can ever be to God.

When you're feeling sorry for those who are giving so much and don't seem to be getting anything in return, take a good look at them and ask yourself some questions: Are they going around complaining all the time? And what about you who consider yourself to have much more than they? Do they look or act worried, frustrated, and fretful—and what about you? Do they appear to be at peace—and what about you, with all that you have? Are they happy in what they are doing—and what about you? Do others admire them, love them, respect them, and call their names blessed—and what about you? Do others feel inspired by being in their presence—and what about you? Do they seem to know what they want out of life—and what about you? They are strong in mind and clear in their thinking—and what about you? Do they have the joy of the Lord—and what about you?

While we're feeling sorry for those who seem to be getting by on meager fare, they're eating every day, getting full, and enjoying their food. Is our gourmet food doing any more for us? While we're feeling sorry for them, look at how they get around physically and do all they do. Look at the shape they're in—and look at some of us. Their homes may not have expensive furnishings, but they enjoy being in them. What about you? Who knows, they may be standing at our grave site feeling sorry for *us* when our casket is being lowered into the ground. If we think their giving hasn't brought them blessings and that God has not kept his word, let's tell them, if we dare, since we're so smart—and we will find out who is not making sense and whose logic is faulty.

"Give and it will be given to you." If this statement doesn't make sense, I would remind you that there is much in our faith that doesn't make sense. The notion of prayer doesn't make sense. Why should a great God hear our feeble voice or be touched by our feeble cries? Why should a God who rules the universe be concerned about our little feeble problems? Yet some of us can witness to the fact that, though the notion of prayer may not make sense, God does hear and answer prayer.

The notion of God's goodness when we continue to neglect God, take God for granted, and break our vows doesn't make sense. Or consider the act of the Incarnation—that God so loved us that God became a human being, that we might have an example of how to live free from the bondage of sin. The notion of God's dying on a cross so that we insignificant human beings might be redeemed from sin—it don't make no sense. The notion that sinful men and women might become equal with angels—it just don't make no sense. Lying Abraham—father of the faithful; conniving Jacob—strives with angels; persecuted Joseph—prime minister of the world's greatest power; lusting David—a man after God's own heart; weeping Jeremiah—God's prophet of strength to a crumbling civilization; Samaritan woman with questionable past—evangel to her people. If God did all these things, we can trust God to keep his word about blessing us in abundant ways when we give.

How much do you trust God? More than the church member in the following story?

A church member was having trouble with the concept of tithing. One day he revealed his doubts to his minister: "Pastor, I just don't see how I can give 10 percent of my income to the church when I can't even keep on top of our bills."

The pastor replied, "John, if I promise to make up the difference in your bills if you should fall short, do you think you could try tithing for just one month?"

After a moment's pause, John responded, "Sure, if you promise to make up any shortage, I guess I could try tithing for one month."

"Now what do you think of that," mused the pastor. "You say you'd be willing to put your trust in a mere man like myself who possesses so little materially, but you couldn't trust your Heavenly Father who owns the whole universe!"

"Give and it will be given." It really does make sense to trust God—who always keeps his word, who always watches out for his own, who feeds the birds and clothes the lilies of the field, who has all power in his hands, who has the whole world in his hands.

It makes sense to trust God, who has the world in his hands.

1. From the play by Melvin Van Peeple, *Ain't Supposed to Die a Natural Death*.

2. James S. Hewett, *Illustrations Unlimited* (Wheaton, Ill.: Tyndale House Publishers, 1988), 461-62.

Bibliography

Fisher, Wallace E. *A New Climate for Stewardship.* Nashville: Abingdon, 1976.

Jones, Clifford A., ed. *From Proclamation to Practice.* Valley Forge: Judson Press, 1993.

Kendall, R. T. *Tithing: A Call to Serious Biblical Giving.* Grand Rapids: Zondervan, 1982.

Knudsen, Raymond B. *Developing Dynamic Stewardship.* Nashville: Abingdon, 1978.

Poovey, W. A. *How to Talk to Christians about Money.* Minneapolis: Augsburg, 1982.

Shannon, Robert C., and Michael J. Shannon. *Stewardship Source Book.* Cincinnati: Standard Publishing, 1987.

Shedd, Charles. *How to Develop a Tithing Church.* Nashville: Abingdon, 1961.

Speaks, R. L. *God in an Age of Scarcity.* Charlotte: A.M.E. Zion Publishing House, 1981.

Walker, Wyatt. *Common Thieves.* New York: Martin Luther King Fellows Press, 1986.

Wimberly, Norma. *Putting God First.* Nashville: Discipleship Resources, 1988.